MW01137639

# FINDING JOY
# AFTER LOSS

## My Journey Through Grief

# FINDING JOY AFTER LOSS

## My Journey Through Grief

**Wendy Benning Swanson**

FINDING JOY AFTER LOSS

My Journey Through Grief

© 2019 by Wendy Benning Swanson

Published by Seeds of the Heart Publishing
St. Paul, MN 55117
(651) 337-8099
www.seedsoftheheartpublishing.com

ISBN: 978-0-578-45597-6

Library of Congress Control Number: 2019901073

Some names and identifying details have been changed
to protect the privacy of individuals.

Printed in the United States of America.

"Goodbyes are only for those who love with their eyes. Because for those who love with their heart and soul, there is no such thing as separation."

— Rumi

To everybody who has experienced loss,
may you find the path to joy...

# Acknowledgments

There are so many people to thank for their love and tireless support over this ten-year journey of the heart. I would like to start with acknowledging Steve's family Dave and JoAnn Benning; Kimberly and Jason Senne; Michael Benning; Scott and Lannette Benning; and Troy Benning, as well as their spouses and extended family members. Thank you for lifting me up out of the deepest of pain and sorrow. Even though you were experiencing it too, you were all a light to guide me to the future and have unwaveringly supported me throughout this journey. I have learned so much from your unconditional love. I would like to acknowledge my friend Julie Milnes, who has been by my side from the beginning, bringing her loving energy to my path. Jodie Harvala and Sunny Dawn Johnston, who have shown me the light and the path through my grief. Chase Michael Benning Swanson, who has been a light guiding me through my pain and suffering with his joy of life. Kayla Swanson, who is a reminder of how life goes on. My husband, Chad Swanson, who has supported me without question through the writing of this book and loves me for all that I am. And finally, my mother Cheryl Bengtson, my late husband Steven Benning, and my father, Gene Bengtson. Witnessing your journeys has taught me about loss and joy and I am forever grateful.

# Table of Contents

# Introduction

When I started the process of writing this book, I didn't know exactly what I was going to write or what format in which I would write it; I just knew that I have learned so much about loss and finding my way out of the darkness and into a place of joy that I wanted to share it with others going through the same thing. I have told my story to many people and often they are thankful because it has given them hope. Hope that maybe they don't have to stay in this place of sadness, loneliness, and darkness forever, and that there is a path back to joy.

There is this feeling of - no, rather a *sense* - of time s.t.o.p.p.i.n.g when you realize that you will never see somebody again. When you see the deceased body of a loved one for the first time, it is a surreal, jarring experience. There lies a human that had love, warmth, a smile, and now it is cold, silent, and dead. Where did they go? You don't know, but you're sure that they've taken a part of you with them. And life is never the same. Period.

My Mom had colon cancer that turned to liver cancer and after about five years of struggling for survival it was time for her to go. I can remember that late September morning so clearly. After several days of sitting vigil at my mother's bedside we had stepped out of the hospice center to go to breakfast. My husband Steve decided to stay with her as my dad, brother, and I went out to eat. We were grateful to be out of the hospice center and around people for a moment, but just as our food arrived, Steve called to tell us that Mom had taken her last breath. We hurried back and as we walked in the room we saw a familiar form lying in the bed. It wasn't my mother, though. Nope. What I saw in that bed was NOT her. Where did she go? Why did she die? Was she in the room right now, watching us? I was three months pregnant with my first child and had the promise of life within me, so I didn't feel I necessarily needed answers to those questions at that moment, but I did ask them, and they would continue to linger.

My son Chase was born on the 22nd of the following February, and my tremendous joy was tempered with sadness that my mother wasn't there. My husband's family did their best to support me, but there is nothing like your mother showing you the ins and outs of what to do when your child is born. I didn't even know how to change a diaper! That first night, not long after Chase was born, Steve left to get something to eat and I had some alone time with him. I looked into his eyes and felt so much love, it was as if I was alive again! I was so tired too! I remember sitting there and holding him and nodding off because I was so exhausted. I remember I just needed to close my eyes for a moment, and then all of a sudden, as I was going to truly fall asleep with him in my arms, and maybe even drop him, I suddenly heard my mother's voice say "WENDY!" I was startled and looked around as if waking from a strange dream. She was here! She was with me! But how? I don't understand? I didn't have the energy to figure it out at the time, but I was grateful that she had come to my rescue.

A little over a year later, on April 27, 2009, my husband passed away from an accidental carbon monoxide poisoning. He had plans to meet a friend that day for a meeting and when he didn't show up the friend came to our house and found him in the garage, sitting in the cab of his truck with a pizza in his lap and vomit down his shirt. There was a window open, but the garage door was shut and the house smelled like smoke and gasoline, the smell that a bad engine gives off. The snowblower was silent but was out of gasoline. The truck was not running either, which makes sense because we know Steve had been working on it and that he was changing the oil at the time. What I believe happened was that he wanted to run the snowblower until it ran out of gas to prepare it for the summer. He started the snowblower, then went inside to get his pizza that had been baking in the oven, and came out and got into his truck to eat it. We don't know when or if he became aware of his dangerous situation, but before he could reach the garage door opener, he had become overcome by the carbon monoxide. Called the "silent killer" because it is odorless and tasteless, carbon monoxide causes confusion, headaches, dizziness, and symptoms similar to those of food poisoning. When it reaches a critical level, victims can lose control of all the muscles in their body. If the levels are lethal, this can happen in only a few minutes. We don't really know what happened that day, but that is the story I tell myself. There was no suicide note and Steve wasn't sad or depressed. The investigators concluded it was not intentional, so that is my belief, it was the timing. He should have opened the garage door first, but for whatever reason he wasn't meant to, because that was the day that he was meant to die.

I was at work when Steve's brother called me to tell me that he was gone. Immediately after calling 911, the friend had called my brother-in-law, who had rushed over to the house. The paramedics tried to revive him, but it was too late. They had no idea how long he had been that way.

At first, I couldn't even understand the words coming out of my brother-in-law's mouth. I do remember running out of my office and to my car to begin the thirty-minute ride home, and I remember that I could barely see because the tears were so heavy. I kept telling myself it wasn't true, it can't be true, how could this have happened to me? How could this have happened to him? Somewhere along the way I placed a hysterical call to my father, who didn't quite understand me but got in the car and drove straight to St. Paul, Minnesota from Cheyenne, Wyoming. I then called a close friend, also in Wyoming, and she booked a flight for the next day. I drove in a daze, it was as if time stood still. I thought about that morning, how I left for work without saying goodbye. Steve had still been sleeping and I felt bad waking him. How could I have known that was the last time I would see him alive?! Then I thought about Chase. I couldn't even go there at that moment; it was too much to bear.

When I finally got home I found policemen and a minister waiting for me; they asked if I wanted to see Steve and I said no. I had seen my mother after she passed and I didn't want to have that memory of my husband. The investigator asked me a couple of questions and the minister asked if I had people to help me, to which I said yes. Then suddenly they were gone and I was alone. The house still smelled like a mixture of gasoline and smoke and was deafeningly silent, so I sat on the front steps with tears pouring down my face and a deep feeling of abandonment flooding my entire being.

People started showing up and they continued to do so throughout the evening. Even more than sadness was an overwhelming feeling of shock. How could someone so wonderful and amazing be taken from us just like that? You see them that morning and they are gone that night. Bam. Without warning. Your life changes in an instant. Nothing can prepare you for this type of sudden, catastrophic loss. Nothing can prepare you for the wake it leaves, for you and everybody else in its path.

When we see bad things happen to others, we do whatever we can to ease their pain. We send them prayers and give them hugs and offer to help them out, all the while thanking God it didn't happen to us. We're grateful, but we don't believe it could happen to us, not *really*. Only then it does happen; someone close to us dies and our foundation cracks and breaks open and we land in a whole new point of life. This is my story. It is a story about loss, and grief, and dealing with my grief and everybody's else's grief, and people's misunderstanding of grief, and how all of it taught me about how important it is to have joy in my life.

# The Black Hole

Even now, I find it difficult to describe the depths of despair you feel when someone you love dies. It's as if life as you know it has stopped and a new, unimaginable one has started. It's different for different kinds of deaths too. Over the five years my mother was sick I think we all went through a sort of grieving process. We knew she was slipping away, and when they said that she only had six months left, we still had the chance to say our goodbyes. When someone dies from an accident there are no goodbyes. When it is your spouse, all your dreams, your hopes, *your life*, collapses in an instant. Gone. That is the black hole. I remember waking up the morning after my husband passed away. I had barely slept - maybe only for a half hour or so – and my first thought was *why?* Why had this happened to us? Why did he have to die, and why did I have to be left alone to raise a one-year-old? Why was a question I would ask for a very long time.

At least I wasn't alone. My friend stayed the night and slept in my bed with me, and I was truly grateful for her presence and that of the others who would be coming that day. They would serve as my strength, and it was enough to bring me out of the hole for the moment. I would worry about the rest later.

So many people came by to give their support those first few days. Some flew in from other parts of the country. Steve was a beloved soul, and as I talked to those who came to grieve their loss, I could feel their deep love for him. We laughed at Steve's humor and told endless "remember that time" stories. One night we all got drunk and, despite our pain, had the best laugh of our lives. Just being together during this painful time gave me hope. It made me feel as if maybe I could get through this.

Then everybody went home…

My father was with me for a short time after the funeral, but his own pain over losing Steve for him was so deep, he couldn't handle it. He went back to Wyoming, and I was alone in my big house with my one-year-old son.

I cried until there were no more tears, but once you are done crying and there are no tears left, you are still alone. Still in a deep, dark cavern of pain that nobody can understand unless they have been there. You go to the depths of your soul and just wonder why? Why did this happen to me? What did I do to deserve this? This wasn't the life I had planned!

I decided to go to a family friend's ranch in Wyoming for a couple of weeks. I had to get out of town; I had to escape the prying eyes and pity I was feeling from everybody; I had to try to wrap my head around what had happened and think about what I was going to do next. I couldn't spend too much time grieving because that was energy I needed give to Chase, our one-year old son. Like all toddlers he was very busy, requiring nearly round-the-clock attention. He was also so happy, which was a blessing, of course, but also confusing. Didn't he miss his dad? I told myself he was only one year old and tried not to think about the gaping hole in his life he would feel later. For the moment, I just appreciated him as a beacon of light that gave me the purpose to get up and get on with my day.

After I had taken care of all the necessary paperwork, my friend drove with me to her family ranch on the Wyoming prairie about thirteen miles outside Newcastle Wyoming, close to the Black Hills of South Dakota. There was barely a tree in sight and you could see for miles and miles. I had gone there for years as a child and thought of the proprietors as my aunt and uncle even though they weren't blood relatives. I had always felt at home there, and now it seemed like the perfect place to escape. Friends that cared for me. A place for Chase to run. I thought, maybe I won't feel such a black hole here. Maybe I will be able to find some light in the midst of this darkness.

The first night was quite rough. After a week of being around a lot of people, many of them strangers, followed by a ten-hour drive, Chase had reached his limit. He didn't ask for his dad but he certainly knew something was off. When I finally got him down the first night it was my first chance to just be alone and to cry. And I cried. I cried to the depths of my soul. I cried for the fact that I wasn't going to see Steve ever again. I cried for Chase that he would never see his father again. How was he going to survive? Was he going to be normal? How was I going to survive? I cried for Steve's parents, how were they going to survive without him? I cried for Steve's close guy friends. He was the glue that brought them all together. I cried for my own dad. I had never seen him so sad. I cried for everyone else that had met Steve and loved him. I could feel their pain and sadness. How could I go on? How could I get up in the morning and take care of Chase when I just wanted to stay in bed…forever? I don't know how long I cried; I think it was hours. Then I somehow found sleep and slept hard for the first time in a week.

Chase got up promptly at six a.m. the next morning. Nobody else was awake yet, and as I sat alone with him, it hit me full-force that this was my new normal as a single parent. It was a club I did not want to be in. I also realized that I had left the baby monitor downstairs, which meant that everyone in the house had heard me crying. Nobody ever said anything to me about it, and I didn't ask; I could only imagine how awful it was for them to hear someone in so much pain and not be able to do anything about it.

Once the day began in earnest, I didn't have much time to think about it. The house wasn't toddler-proof, so I was on constant vigil, chasing Chase around, making sure he didn't knock things over or get into things he shouldn't. Nobody was there to take a shift or to give me a break, either. They had a working ranch, and everyone was off feeding and tending to the animals, going to appointments or events or generally going about their business. Their lives were going on as normal. I knew it was out of necessity, but it brought little comfort. I felt as if I was stuck in time and space. How could everybody go on? How come time didn't stop for them too? How come they weren't weeping all night and not wanting to get out of bed? How was the sun still rising and falling each day?

Chase loved it there. There was so much for him to do and explore. I, on the other hand, felt trapped. He needed constant attention and I wanted to just go to sleep, I wanted to go hide, but there was nobody to relieve me. Everybody was working or busy.

One afternoon thier daughter asked if I wanted to go to a branding party at her friend's ranch. It sounded interesting, something to do, so I said yes. What an experience! This particular ranch still performed traditional branding, which meant that they had horsemen and calf ropers and people had to physically wrestle the calves to the ground to put the brand on them. It was fascinating to watch and a much-needed chance to get out of my own head for a while. Even Chase ceased his non-stop action long enough to watch the cowboys with me. There was one moment in particular that stood out to me. Two girls about five or six years old were playing nearby. One girl asked the other who I was and why I was there, and her friend replied that my husband/Chase's dad had died. Then they both looked over and saw me standing there with eyes as wide as saucers. Aside from the embarrassment that I'd overheard them, I could also sense something else coming from them, and that something was pity. At that moment I could tell the girls were looking at Chase and wondering what it would be like to lose a dad. I sensed their fear for themselves, of the possibility of loss, and even concern for me and how I would handle life alone. After all I had been through, I didn't think I could feel any worse. That changed the moment I saw five-year-old's pitying me. Little did I know this would be the first of many such experiences. For the next few years, pity would be a presence in nearly every interaction I had with almost everyone who knew of my circumstances. *Oh, poor Wendy…how is she going to survive? I'm so glad that I'm not her.* I would see and feel it in the eyes of family and friends; I would hear it in the voices of the people from my job who said that they were going to stop by but didn't. I knew that they didn't know how to show up. They couldn't imagine being me, losing their spouse; they didn't know what to say or how to say it and thought it was better to stay away than say something wrong. It was the same thing I had seen in those five-year-old's' faces. Though they didn't yet have the capacity to fully grasp the situation, they were thinking, *what do I say to her? Get me out of here!*

The most beautiful thing my friends on the ranch did for me on that trip was to show me zero pity, only kindness and respect. Upon reflection I decided this was because they lived on a ranch. They saw life begin and end all the time, albeit with animals, and therefore had a different perspective than most. Even from my dark space, I knew I wanted a better understanding of that perspective.

I stayed at the ranch through Memorial Day, when friends and family gathered together for the long weekend. This was a tradition that we'd carried on since I was a child. I was still in shock and in survival mode, but it was a nice distraction. The thing that struck me was how nobody wanted to talk to me about what happened. Each of them had been at the funeral, but now they were acting as if it were any other Memorial Day. Outwardly, I went along with it; on the inside, I felt like I was dying. All I wanted to do was stay in bed, but I couldn't because I had to take care of Chase. I might have asked for help, but this group wasn't really around children much, they were about let's pick ourselves up and move on, and there hadn't been an infant/toddler in the house for many years. I wanted desperately to escape and be alone, but I didn't see any possibility of that in the near future.

To make things worse, at some point that weekend I bit into something hard and the filling, from a bicycle accident as a child, on my front tooth came out. A quarter of my front tooth was gone. Not only was the tooth sharp, it was very embarrassing to smile. *WHAT?* Here I was, in the middle of the prairie on Memorial Day weekend, in the proverbial "middle of nowhere" so there is no way it could be fixed any time soon. Why was all of this happening to me? WHY??? I felt as if I was being punished for something. It was an additional blow to an already unbelievably stressful situation. My only shining light was Chase. He was happy, and he certainly didn't care about my tooth. I think he was the only reason I kept it together the rest of that weekend.

I returned home a couple of days later. It was first time in a month that I wasn't surrounded by people. The house was dark, but I was grateful to be in a space without pity for a while. I had a list of things to take care of, the first being getting my tooth fixed. Immediately I thought, *how am I going to tell them that Steve died?* The thought was unbearable, but I had no choice but to go. I thought about just *not* telling them, but they had already been calling and telling me that Steve needed to get his teeth cleaned and I didn't want that anymore either. When I called, they told me they could squeeze me in right away that morning. I sat there with my mouth open, dreading the moment that I would have to tell them. WHY? Why did I have to go through this? Why me? Why Why Why??? Why can't I catch a break? How did this happen to me?

These thoughts swirled through my mind the entire time they worked on my tooth. Finally, I decided I'd tell the office manager on my way out. After I paid, I said, "Um, by the way, can you remove my husband Steve from your records? He recently passed away."

The look on her face was a mix of, *what do I do or say? How terrible for her?,* and *I'm glad it's not me.* She was gracious enough, but I knew that experience was as bad for me as it was for her.

The next thing was to decide what to do with the house. My husband had remodeled it, but it had a high mortgage and I just wanted to get as far away from it as I could. Fortunately, I wasn't on the mortgage, so I was able to walk away from it without any repercussions. It was 2009 in the midst of the recession, so we wouldn't have been able to sell it for what the mortgage was on it anyway.

Chase was back in daycare and my job had said I could take more time off, so I was able to look around for another place for us to live. Sure enough, I found an apartment not too far away with two bedrooms and a parking space. I moved in a couple of weeks later with Chase and my two cats Maverick and Indiana. About a week after I moved in, Indiana, the cat Steve had gotten me before we were married, started acting really strange. He wouldn't eat and when I came home from work, he was just lying on the ground growling. My friends were out of town and my in-laws were about two hours away, so I called my brother-in-law to watch Chase so I could take Indiana to the emergency vet. I didn't have a good feeling as I was driving him there. *Please don't do this to me,* I begged silently, *this is my friend, my companion, my loving gift from my husband, please make sure he is okay.*

When we got there, the vet said that it didn't look good. He took some bloodwork and then we had to wait. As I waited, I talked to Indiana and told him to hang in there, that I needed him to stay with me. But it was not to be. The vet came back and gave me the awful news: Indiana was dying. He didn't have much of a chance of survival and his recommendation was that I put him down. WHAT?! This was my buddy, one of my best friends. He was what was getting me through. I knew that I didn't want him to suffer so I said okay. I sat there crying my eyes out as the vet administered the drug. I was mad. No, I was beyond mad, I felt betrayed. I didn't know why all of this was happening to me, why everyone seemed to be leaving me. I was in the depths of despair, the black hole.

The vet's staff was gracious and gave me some time alone with Indiana, but what was the point? He was gone, somewhere else now, so I left. I got in my car and just sat there and felt so sad, so alone, and so lost. It really was the lowest I had ever felt. The best way to describe it is like being at the bottom of a pit so deep and dark you can't see your way out.

Then, suddenly, I heard, *Indy is with me now, he's okay. You are going to be okay.*

I felt a tingling that started in my toes and slowly went up through my feet, my legs, my body, my arms, all the way to the top of my head, and all of a sudden, I felt hope again. I felt light. I felt okay to move on. It was as if my sadness was heard and answered with a physical manifestation of love from beyond this time and place. It was grace. It was what I absolutely needed at that moment. I drove home and felt okay with what happened and I knew that it was going to be okay.

# Managing Other People's Grief

The most surprising thing about being part of this new club was that often I had to support others in their grief and sadness. In fact, I did more of it than anyone did for me. It boggled my mind. I can see it from such a different place now, but at the time it was quite irritating. And not only did I have to manage their grief, I had to manage how they *thought* I should be grieving. My sense was that most of what people knew about grief or how a spouse of the deceased should grieve is what they had seen on TV and in the movies. I sensed that people thought I should be withdrawn, sitting in a corner with a long black dress and a hat with a black veil on it. Honestly, if I was in their shoes, I probably would have thought the same thing. But that is not how it works, at least not in my case. I was the sole caregiver of a happy, active toddler, so I didn't have much choice but to get my butt out of bed every morning to take care of him. I also decided that I was going to go back to work for at least a year. I felt it was best to have some sort of normalcy while adjusting to life without my husband.

About six weeks after Steve's death, my boss called and asked when I would be coming back. He wasn't very compassionate, and there was an underlying tone of, "It's been long enough, are you coming back or not?", rather than, "How are you doing?" I gave him a date, then hung up the phone wondering how was I going to do this. How was I going to face everyone?

I worked for a national staffing agency as a sales executive and had been there for about five years at the time. My husband was well known and liked at my company; in fact, just two months before his death we had returned from a President's Club contest party in Cancun, which I earned and where we spent a lot of time hanging out with my colleagues. Many of those same people had attended his wake and funeral. A few of them reached out to me while I was out, but not many. Now I wondered, what are they going to say? How are they going to treat me? How was I going to act? I tried to focus on the positive, that I was looking forward to having something else to look forward to every day, something to put my mind on, something else to focus on.

I'll never forget walking into the office that first day back. As I walked through the door it was as if there was a spotlight on me and everybody turned to look at me and didn't say anything. It felt like a walk of shame. I could feel most people's discomfort at seeing me and not knowing what to say to me. I knew they were thinking about what they would do in my shoes, and that they didn't understand how I could even be there.

I walked directly into my office, feeling annoyed, saddened and angry, yet at the same time I also felt empathy for their discomfort because I was feeling it too. At our morning meeting, attended by everyone in the office, there was a passing recognition that I was back and that was it, which was fine. I'm not one to have a lot of attention on me. But I was bothered by the palpable tension in the room.

Throughout the day people diverted their eyes from me. Most didn't ask how I was doing, and others tried to ignore me altogether. It was pretty terrible. The office manager didn't

really say much to me, but it would have been nice if he prepared people for my arrival. It wasn't their fault that they didn't
know what to say or do - I get that now - but a warmer welcome
would have made a big difference in my life at the time.

The next hurdle was dealing with my clients. I remember sitting down at my desk and being in such a different place than I
was when I left. How could I do this job? I still needed to work to
provide for my son, but I had little desire or motivation to check
in with my current clients or set up meetings with potential ones.
To make matters worse, we were heading into a recession, which
made it difficult to find new business. On the other hand, when
they first heard about Steve's death, my current clients had sent
me the most beautiful letters and flowers and notes. They were
heartfelt and open and raw. I had always believed in separating
my personal and professional life, but I realized that there was no
separation. They cared about me, more than my own colleagues,
and though I wanted to thank them I dreaded making the calls. I
just wanted to be home in bed with the covers over my face, not
out in the real world dealing with people's perceptions of me. It
was one of the most difficult experiences of my life.

I decided to avoid them for the time being and instead spent
the next couple of weeks cold-calling potential new clients.
Eventually, though, I no longer had a choice; my clients had
needs and I had to address them. The conversations generally
went like this: They would ask, "How are you?" to which I would
give my stock answer, "I'm okay." This would be followed by, "I
don't know how you can be back at work"; to which I would say,
"I know, it is hard"; then they would say, "I don't know what I
would do in your shoes"; and I would say, "Oh, it will be okay";
or they would ask, "How are you surviving?"; to which I would
reply, "I'm surviving day by day" or something along those lines.

I had so many variations of this dialogue that eventually I lost count. Suffice it to say it was typical of most conversations I had during those first weeks and months. Every time someone said "I don't know what I would do in your shoes" it was like a bullet shot through my heart. I wanted to say, "I don't know what I am doing in my shoes! This is new to me! I wake up every morning alone and get ready for work alone and am taking care of my son alone and go shopping alone and live alone and everything and everyone keeps going. And I'm slowly dying inside every day, but I have to go back to work." But of course, I didn't, I just said whatever would end the conversation the fastest. I realized later that when people said those things, it was simply because they didn't know what else to say.

Before long I realized that I had become the soother as they tried to process their own feelings. While visiting Cheyenne for the fourth of July, I saw a friend that I hadn't seen in years but knew Steve well. As soon as he saw me, he started crying, then weeping uncontrollably. I sat down with him and patted his back as he went on and on about how much he liked Steve and how he couldn't believe he was gone, et cetera. It was a little over two months since Steve's death and by then I had become pretty good with people like this, telling them "it will be okay"; that "I understood where they were coming from"; and even that I knew it was hard to see me. This happened on and off for the first year. I would randomly see people and they would get upset and I would find myself in the role of comforter. And even as I did so I was thinking, why *am I soothing them? Why can't anybody soothe me?* For the most part, I knew these people only thought about Steve's death when they saw me; I was dealing with it every single moment of every single day. As time went on, I realized that I was far beyond them in them grieving process which in and of itself was both heartening and upsetting.

Other people said things that almost sounded as if I should feel guilty for trying to move on. I had been back to work for about a month when my office manager announced he was having a summer party at his house. My brother-in-law was taking Chase for the day, so I decided to go. I thought it would be good to see people again. I thought this up until the moment I was cornered in the garage by my manager's wife, a woman I knew fairly well but was not close with. What began as the usual "How are you doing?", "I'm okay," interaction then went off the rails. "Oh my gosh, Wendy," she gushed, "I don't know how you are surviving, there is no way that I could survive what you went through, I mean how do you even get up in the morning? I think I would just want to die, I would move away to another country and never come back. How do you get up in the morning?" It was like being hit by a runaway train.

When she finally paused, I said simply, "I have to get up for my son."

"Well good for you, I don't think I could do it, how are you even back to work, how can you work? We are all wondering why you are here."

It went on and on like that, and it was horrible.

I waited until she finally came up for air again, then I excused myself and went home, feeling more alone than ever. *They didn't know why I was back at work?* Clearly it hadn't occurred to them that at least it forced me to get up in the morning. Something that allowed me to feel like I was moving forward, even though it was extremely painful to do so. And as for the woman, she had used the conversation to unload some of her own junk, things that had nothing to do with me. Why was she throwing all of that up on me? I was annoyed at her rudeness, yet at the same time I was sure she didn't realize she was doing it to me.

Why does the person grieving have to manage everybody else's grief? Why do we have it backwards? Over time and after several hundred conversations, I realized that as a society or a culture we don't teach people how to communicate with someone who has suffered a traumatic loss. We don't talk about grief and death, we don't know how to grieve or what it even is for us, or how to diagnose it. We don't understand that grief is a natural response to loss. Sure, most people understand it on a superficial level, they think of it as a passing phase that everyone goes through at some point or another. But they don't understand it from the physical, cognitive, behavioral, social, cultural, spiritual and philosophical dimensions. This is in part because many people, at least not in my world, have ever lost someone that young and close to them; it is not something they have prepared for or even seriously thought about.

What I have learned is that we grieve when we feel loss, when there is some sort of irrevocable change to some aspects of our lives. This is not limited to a death, and can include the loss of a relationship, a job, a pet, or a friendship. Even a positive change in circumstances, such as retirement, moving to a new, desirable place, or getting a new job can spark a grieving period. Grieving is a natural part of our human nature. But everybody grieves differently. I know people who have lost a spouse ten years ago and are still deep into the grieving process and may never recover. I have seen friends go through divorces and find themselves unable to get over losing their spouse to another. I have seen grief wipe all happiness from families and friends. The thing is, everybody will die, everyone will experience loss, and change is constant. Grief is unavoidable.

# Steve and Me. Us.

Steve and I met the first weekend of my first year of college. I had come from Cheyenne, Wyoming to attend a small private school in St. Paul, Minnesota. Steve had also come to St. Paul from a small town in central Minnesota and was attending another small private college nearby. During my college orientation, my fellow freshman and I were bused over to his school for a dance. My college was an all woman's college, so we were all very excited about an opportunity to meet some boys.

The evening began with boys standing on one side of the room and girls on the other. The music was playing, but no one was willing to get out there and dance. Later, I would learn that Steve's friends had been at football practice most of the day and were exhausted. Steve, who was not playing that year, was all revved up and ready to go. When they saw me drag a couple of girls onto the dance floor, they apparently dared him to ask me to dance.

At first, I was reluctant to dance with this young man who shot across the floor toward me, but then his friends came over and asked my friends to dance and before I knew it, we were all having a great time. Later that night Steve asked for my phone number. I couldn't even remember what it was because it was my dorm room phone number (we didn't have cell phones at the time), so I gave him my email address and left feeling like I was on cloud nine. Less than a week in town and already I had met someone cute and fun to hang out with. It was like a dream come true.

For the next year, Steve and I would spend most of our free time together. I even went up to his parents' house for Thanksgiving. I loved that he had a big family and they were all friendly and welcoming to me. A month later, over January break, Steve came out to Wyoming for a week. It was his first time on an airplane.

We had so much fun that year that by the time spring semester ended I knew he was the one. That summer Steve's family bought a house in St. Paul for him and his brothers and friends to live in while they were in school. Steve moved back home for the summer to help at the family construction business, and since I didn't have anywhere to live, he said I could live in the new house with his friends until school started up again. Everything seemed perfect.

However, the unthinkable happened right before the start of the football season. I had about a week left in the house before I could move to my dorm room. I had fun over the summer, but I was looking forward to going back to school and especially for Steve coming back to town. Imagine my shock when upon returning he promptly broke up with me. It was getting a little too serious for him. I was beyond crushed at losing him; I was also beyond humiliated that for the next week, I had to live in that house with all of his friends. That schoolyear mostly went by in a blur, for even after I started to recover from the breakup I didn't have nearly as much fun as I had with Steve, and I spent my junior year at a University in Tasmania, Australia. I had moved on with my life and even dated a couple of other people, but it was never the same.

I had one semester of college left before graduating after I returned from Australia. I wasn't sure what I was going to do next. I got a job for the summer at the University of Minnesota Ecological Research Station doing field work on their long-term ecological projects. When that ended, I had no job or plans for the rest of my life. I decided to move back to Wyoming to figure out my next steps. Before I left, I contacted my friends that I had made through Steve to say goodbye because I assumed that I wasn't coming back to Minnesota. One of them said that he was hoping I would call because he had an invitation for me to his wedding and it had just been sent back to them. He forwarded it to me. The wedding was on the Saturday before the Monday that I left Minnesota to move back home with my parents. I had a feeling I would see a lot of people I hadn't seen in a long time, including Steve and possibly his family. Since I was moving home, I figured why not go and see what happens. My last chance to maybe reconnect with him. Is he dating someone? Is he married? I hadn't had an update on what he was doing or where he was for a couple of years since I had been out of the country. It was a little nerve-wracking because my friends were all busy and they couldn't come with me at such short notice, so I attended solo. It was a couple of hours out of town in Red Wing, so I had to rent a hotel room for the evening. As I was driving, I was wondering why I was even going. I hadn't seen many of these people for several years and I'm going alone. I could envision a lot of opportunity for awkward moments. There were a couple of times that I seriously considered turning back towards home on my way there. Nobody would know or care one way or the other. But I really did want to put an end note to my relationship with Steve. I could leave at any moment if it was uncomfortable and deep down, I wanted to see him one last time before I was gone forever.

When I arrived at the wedding, everyone was happy to see me since it had been years since I had seen them. Steve's family was all there and there were lots of hugs and catching up. Steve's twin had a fiancé now and his siblings were all kind enough to hang out with me. Steve and I said hello and had our pleasantries but didn't speak too much. I hadn't seen some of our friends for years, so it was a fun evening of catching up with everybody and enjoying the food and dancing. Steve was there, but we really didn't chat, I was busy catching up with everybody and somewhat avoiding him. What was I going to say? What were we going to talk about? I went back to the hotel room after the reception was over and thought that I wished I could have talked to Steve more. I was sitting watching TV when there was a knock at my door. I opened it and Steve was there! We went to the lobby and spend the evening and early morning talking until 4 a.m. I told him I was moving home, and he told me that he wasn't dating anybody. We enjoyed catching up and I headed home later that morning.

The next day I drove back to Wyoming, not at all sure how I felt. I had a great evening with Steve, and I got the feeling that he was still interested in me. I on the other hand, I couldn't forget that he had broken my heart before. When I got back to Wyoming, Steve started calling me every day. We didn't have cell phones back then, so he would call my parent's house. My mother was thrilled. She had always adored Steve and was as bummed as I was when we broke up. He would call her to chat and to see when I would be home and even whether she thought I would ever consider moving back to Minnesota. Sometimes I thought the two of them were conspiring to get us back together. It seemed fate was conspiring as well. Shortly after I moved home, I received an email from my boss at the University of Minnesota asking whether I would be interested in a full-time job at the research center. It was a no-brainer; I had enjoyed my work there and I had no opportunities in Cheyenne at the time. I told him I was very interested, and we decided that I should start in the spring when the research center got busy. Steve and I officially got back together not long after I moved back to Minnesota and we dated for couple of years before we were married in August of 2001.

Steve's greatest quality was his ability to make people laugh. Just recently someone told me that making someone laugh is one of the greatest gifts you can give people. It can shift them from wherever they are in life into happiness. Laughter can clear a whole room of negative energy in an instant, especially when the humor is funny without disparaging others. That's how Steve's brand of humor was, and I always loved to observe how he could shift people's energy with just a few jokes and well-placed smiles. People loved to spend time with him because they always left him feeling better than they had when they arrived. He was also amazing with children and was gifted with the ability to connect with them on their level. Most children loved being around him as much as adults did, and no one loved it more than our own son. I remember one night, not long before he passed away. Chase was sitting at the island in our kitchen and Steve pretended that he tripped and then was hopping around on one leg and looking at Chase. Chase was laughing so hard, he could barely breathe. I stood there, recording this beautiful moment together, never imaging that he would soon be gone. That video serves as a reminder to savor every precious moment with our loved ones because we never know when it will be the last.

Steve had a wonderful group of friends, the closest of whom were the guys he had grown up with and gone to college with. But he also had different groups of people that he would connect and weave together. Steve had a way of making people feel comfortable with each other. If we were out dancing, he would make funny dancing moves and get everybody in the group on the dance floor doing them. We all would laugh so hard our sides ached. He was always doing things that nobody in their right minds would do but were so bad, so irreverent, that people couldn't help but laugh. I think that is how humor works, making people look that things differently, or in a way that is fantastic, implausible or even silly. I was fascinated by Steve's ability to do this. I would ask all the time, "Where did that come from?" and he would say, "I don't know, it just popped in my head." Wherever they came from, Steve's hijinks never failed bringing unforgettable moments of joy to the people in his life.

# Finding the strength to move on – One. Day. At. A. Time.

Steve's funeral was in April, but we waited until later that summer to spread his ashes around Rim Lake, the lake in Wyoming that his company was named after. Located deep in the mountains, it is only accessible about three months of the year and one month, August, when it is warm enough to enjoy. Still, it was quite a trek for our family and friends to attend. In total we had over twenty people journey to the Dubois, Wyoming area, many of whom who had never been to the mountains before. The preparation was intense - four-wheelers were needed, along with camping gear for all types of weather and I was lucky to have friends helping me get everyone situated.

Though I put on a good front for people, I felt like I was dying inside. *How am I doing this?* I asked myself, *Steve and I should be going here to enjoy a week of camping; I shouldn't be here, in this beautiful place, spreading his ashes!*

I had prepared something lovely to say for the event, but I didn't want to go. I didn't want to be there. I didn't want anything to do with it. I was tired of dealing with it. I was tired of dealing with other people's grief, or of them not understanding what I was going through.

Finally, the day arrived. The lake was quite a distance from our main camping spot, about an hour and a half ride in on our off-road vehicles, followed by another hour on foot. It was quite the experience to get everybody there that day. It wasn't until we headed off that I realized it was our wedding anniversary. Steve and I were married on August 4, 2001 and I was going to spread his ashes on August 4, 2009. All the pain and loss I thought I had been dealing with came back full force, so much so that it almost brought me to my knees. Even though I was surrounded by family and friends, I had never in my life felt so alone. Though each was in their own state of pain, none of them could relate to what I was going through. Nobody there had had to experience it; they were all there with their spouses, who were alive and well. Why did this happen to me? Did I do something to deserve this? Why was this happening on this particular date? Why did the universe set this up this way? To torture me?

When we finally made it to the lake, it took every ounce of strength to read what I had written.

> *I wasn't able to say anything during the visitation or funeral and I wanted the opportunity to share some of my thoughts about Steve and the both of us and the location that he chose to have his ashes placed. When Steve and I reunited after being apart for four years back in 1999, I invited him to go on this camping trip. It was nerve-wracking because this place is so special to me, my family, and our friends, and it was kind of a test to see whether he could take it and get along with everybody. I really had my doubts because he had never done anything like this before, and if he didn't like it, it may have been a deal breaker. Well, as always, Steve made the*

*most of it and had a great time. I'm not sure if he fell in love with it that trip or if he learned to love it over time, but through the years I saw how excited he was to take this trip, how he described it to everyone, and I knew that he loved it as much if not more than I did. When it comes to Rim Lake, I think he loved it because he found a lake that, in the twenty-five years our families have come here, we had never found which meant it was "his lake", I think he loved it because he was so competitive with Ann Marie that he was sure it would have bigger and better fish…and it did, I think he loved it because it was a place that he could bring people and they could have a good chance of catching the biggest fish, and it would be worth all of the effort to get here. I think he loved it because it was the one place in the world that nobody could get a hold of him by phone and he could truly be at peace.*

*In July of 2000 Steve proposed to me on the top of the mountain above Horseshoe Lake. Today is our eight- year anniversary. I can't help but wonder why it has worked out that way, but I do believe that things happen for a reason, so the symbolism can't be denied. Maybe it's a sign that the mountains are where his ashes belong, and maybe there is some comfort in that. What I do know is that he loved it here.*

*We had a great life, and I will cherish the memories forever. In the time that he has passed away, there have been countless instances where people have described how much they are a better person because of Steve. That doesn't surprise me, because he made me a better person every day. But it is a testament to who he was. He was someone that cared more about the people around him than himself. He went out of his way to make people happy and never asked for anything in return. I have learned so much from his selflessness and positivity that I only hope that I can teach that way of life to Chase. We are all better people because he was in this world.*

*Now it is time to say goodbye to his physical remains. We don't need to say goodbye to his spirit, because it is around us every day. He is now an angel watching over us and I'm sure he continues to do everything he can to help all of us. I just want to say I love you Steve, I will do my best to take care of Chase and make sure that he grows up to be a strong, kind, and happy man. And, I will never forget you or what we had together, because it was an amazing life that most people would be lucky to have lived. I love you.*

Those words ring just as true today as the day I spoke them. And though I still haven't figured out why the date we spread his ashes coincided with the day we were married, I do know that was probably my lowest point.

My friend and I had packed a tent and supplies for one night's stay at Rim Lake while everybody else went back to the camping spot. We burned the urn until it was ash and then I went to sleep, ready to move forward.

It was only later that I looked back on that day and recalled several synchronicities that could only have been signs from Steve. After we were done with our small ceremony, we all fished that lake, and everybody had a lot of fun catching bigger fish, just as Steve would have wanted it. Even in August the lake wasn't normally that warm, and it usually took someone fishing it hard to get any of the big ones to take the lures, so this was unique. The whole experience felt like his gift to us. Odder still was the big eagle feather found on a rock next to us. Since Steve's funeral several people, including his mother and his best friend, had found random feathers in places they shouldn't have been, but I didn't really believe in that. I had an analytical, science-based mindset and I didn't understand how a feather could be strategically placed so that I would find it and I certainly didn't think that it would be from my deceased husband. Still, I knew they believed these feathers were from Steve, so the feather's presence on the rock that day was a notable occurrence.

When I returned home, I felt a sense of completion, and a sense that it was time to start to consider life without Steve. My first goal, though, was to get through one year, as I had read that the hardest part of a spouse's death is going through all the seasons, holidays, and parties alone. The day to day was difficult enough. Luckily, I had Chase to care for, and Steve's family was still an important part of my life. I tried to distract myself in any way I could. My friend Julie had given me Outlander, a thick historical fiction novel. Each night after Chase was asleep, I would curl up with it and escape the reality of being a single mother with a stressful sales job.

I found that one of the hardest things to do was attending weddings alone. One wedding in particular should have been amazing, if only because it was taking place in Hawaii. Instead it turned out to be a nightmare. Everybody had a significant other with them and their happiness served as a million reminders of my own situation. I wished more than anything that Steve could be there with me, that we could be one of those laughing couples out on the dancefloor, but the reality was that he wasn't there, and he would never be again. It was a reminder that I was alone in this world and the future was unknown. I did my best to put on a happy face, but I was deeply grieving and mourning the loss of my life as I had known it, and the path to the future I had planned.

One day, everyone else was off with their significant others on some fun adventure, so I decided to hang out on the beach in front of the hotel. I thought, this should be fine, I'll just relax by myself, but as I sat there, I couldn't help but notice all the couples walking by. It occurred to me at that moment that most of these people were probably here for their honeymoon, their anniversary or some romantic event. It broke my heart. Would I ever again be walking on the beach with someone? Sitting there made me feel more alone than ever, yet for some reason I stayed there for a while, watching the endless parade of couples walking by. I should have been having fun in this tropical paradise, but I wasn't because I was still so deep in grief that I couldn't see any light in my darkness.

Christmas was another major hurdle the first year. Just walking into Steve's family's house knowing he wouldn't be there was both surreal and agonizing. Steve had a large nuclear family that included four siblings, and an even larger extended family, as his father was one of twelve and his mother was one of four, so holidays were always joyous affairs. Or had been. Eight months after Steve's death we were all still heavily grieving but trying to make the best of things. I knew everyone was struggling, but as I looked around, I couldn't help but think, *At least they all still have their spouses. I am alone.*

We had a lovely dinner and played some games. Alcohol was flowing, and everyone's spirits seemed to lift. I tended to Chase and played along and put on my usual brave face. Then Steve's mom reached for one of those games where each person gets a bunch of letters and has to use them to form words. When she opened the box, there, sitting on top, was a feather. She was so excited, saying it was another sign from Steve, reminding us that he was with us for the holidays. Though I was admittedly surprised to see it, I found it hard to believe it was a sign. How could Steve have put a feather in a box? The logistics didn't make sense to me.

Shortly after discovering the feather, I decided to turn in. It was way past Chase's bedtime and all the laughter was painful for me. I held it together while we said our goodnight then burst into tears as I got into bed. It wasn't because I could still hear everybody laughing – I much preferred that to tears – but because Steve and I weren't down there laughing with them. I couldn't laugh like that right now. It wasn't in my heart. Sometimes I thought I would never be able to laugh like that again. Would I ever have another joy-filled Christmas? At that moment the answer felt like a resounding no. I couldn't see it, I couldn't picture it, it was just blackness. I tried to find a silver lining, something to be grateful for, and I did: Steve's family was still welcoming to me; in fact, they had been my biggest support system. But even this didn't dull the pain at all, it was just a speck of light that allowed me to fall asleep that evening after crying so hard I didn't have any tears left.

Even as I tried to accept Steve's absence, I was looking for some evidence that maybe he was still around. I did believe this, but I also didn't. I guess I just didn't know. A couple of months after Steve passed, I was at a restaurant near my house and saw the man who ministered Steve's funeral and his wife. They knew Steve personally because he had remodeled their house about a year before and they had adored working with him, both for his sense of humor and his impeccable custom work. As we chatted, they excitedly told me the story of a grey feather that was on their driveway not long after Steve's funeral. *Here we go again,* I thought, *another feather.* They proceeded to tell me that there had been a feather in that exact spot the whole time he had been working on their house. They had noticed it at the time and thought it was odd but didn't think too much about it... until the feather appeared in the same spot after the funeral. They knew in their hearts that it was from Steve.

I thanked them for the story, told them how lovely that was, but deep down I still had a hard time believing that Steve could put a feather in a particular spot for them to see. It didn't make any sense to me. My heart wanted to believe it, but my analytical mind kept saying, Lovely *thought, but no. Not possible.*

Not long after that, one of Steve's friends told me he found a feather on a window sill inside his house. He had no idea how it got there, but he was sure it was from Steve. *Okay, that is interesting, but I'm still not convinced.* Steve's mother told me of a time when she found a feather in her house and that was very nice, but I still didn't connect to it. I wondered, will I ever get my sign?

One evening I was curled up with one of my copies of the Outlander series, just as I had been so many nights before. Chase was with his cousins for the weekend, so I was alone in the apartment. I'm not sure why, but the book triggered something in me and I was having a terrible cry. A deep ugly cry, one of those ugly cries that you know will leave you all red and puffy-looking. Suddenly, my home phone rang. I looked at the clock and saw that it was eleven p.m. How odd. People rarely called that number, and certainly not at that hour. I went down to pick it up and heard only static. About five minutes later it rang again, and this time I let it go to voicemail. When I listened to the voicemail it was the same static. Maybe the phone company was doing testing? Or maybe someone was trying to call me, but it wasn't coming through? No, they would have called my cell phone, not my home phone. There were several possible explanations, but I couldn't help but feel there was something more to it than that. The thought flashed through my mind that maybe this was Steve trying to reach out to me through time and space, but I quickly dismissed it. That would be a far too easy explanation. It had to be something else. But what? I really tried to think of an explanation. Nobody had ever called that phone. Maybe it was Steve. I thought back to the moment when the phone had first rung. I was so deep in grief. I was feeling overwhelmed, lost, feeling like there was no future for me, feeling like I couldn't be a great single parent, feeling that I didn't want to be alone for the rest of my life. Like I didn't know how to move forward. I was still wearing my wedding ring and didn't know when I should take it off. That phone call had jolted me out of my pit of despair. And for some reason, it gave me hope. The timing of it was *so* perfect. It was another one of my lowest moments.

Was it a coincidence, or was it a sign that Steve was actually listening to me and could hear my grief and that he didn't want to see me crying? Was he telling me that the future was going to be fine, that I would find happiness again, and that this was all part of a greater plan? These thoughts crossed my mind and I held on to them with hope for a moment. A beautiful pure moment. But it couldn't be true. How could he communicate with me through the phone? How embarrassing that

I even contemplated that! No, it was a lovely coincidence, but a useful one. My crying spell had stopped, and I was able to get some sleep.

The next day a friend and I met for lunch at an outdoor café in St. Paul. It was a lovely day and we were going shopping for bridesmaids' dresses for her upcoming wedding. During lunch I happened to look down at my feet and there, right next to them, was a large white feather. Even after all the feather stories I might have dismissed it, but the phone calls the night before gave me pause. *Where did this feather come from? I don't see any birds around.* It was a fairly large feather too, seemingly too large for the sort of birds usually seen in the area. My mind was racing for an explanation of how this feather got here, but there really was no explanation other than it was a coincidence…or maybe not? Maybe this really was a sign? A sign of what, though? That Steve was there? That he was watching over me? How did that work? I wasn't sure, but it did give me a small bit of hope that maybe I wasn't alone. Maybe there was something more after we die, and it was reaching out to me. It was a small little nugget of hope, but it was something to hold on to. It was something to give me more purpose than I had up to this point. A reason to keep moving. Because if it was true, I didn't want to disappoint him! If he was really trying to reach out to me, I wanted to make him proud and show him that I could do this. I could survive this without him and make sure that Chase grew up to be a strong, successful, and happy man.

# What do you do with your wedding ring? Till death do us part?

Of the many things that plagued me that first year was the question of how long I was supposed wear my wedding ring. How long before it seemed weird? Did people even notice? Did that matter? I thought about the wedding vows that say, "Till death do us part," the vows that say that I will love and protect you, be true to only you, and so on, with the understanding that you are both still living. How did this work now that he was gone? I still loved him, and our wedding ring symbolized that, so if I take it off does that mean that I don't love him anymore? That didn't feel true, but there was something about the tradition of the wedding and the ring that I struggled with. Taking it off meant he was really gone. That our wedding vows were null and void. The end. It just seemed so…final. So cold. So mean. So uncaring. It's hard to explain, and there was no one for me to talk to anyway. I didn't know anybody other than my father who had lost a spouse, and it wasn't really a topic that he and I discussed.

The toughest thing was that I felt like taking off the ring was my symbolically telling the universe that I was ready to love someone else. I didn't know when or if that would ever happen, but just the thought brought up a whole host of other questions. Like, could I love someone else without decreasing my love for Steve? Was love like a pie - you only have so much and if most of the pie is given to one person there is only a tiny portion left for someone else? And if you give half of the pie to one and half of the pie to another, does that mean that the other person isn't going to have the opportunity to have the full you? Is that how it will be? That was my mentality at the time. Taking off my ring was like telling the world that I was done with Steve and ready for someone else, which just seemed wrong in so many ways. I would never be "done" with Steve. How are you "done" with someone you love, just because they are no longer in physical form?

Finally, I decided that I was going to wear my ring until I felt like it was time to remove it. I don't recall exactly how long that was, but I do remember feeling like people had started noticing it. They were all wondering the same thing. *Is she still wearing the ring?* I could feel that they were judging me, thinking I was stuck in the past and needed to move on. I also knew that If I hadn't been wearing the ring, they would have thought I was moving on too quickly and how could I do that to Steve? It was like I couldn't win no matter what I did. I eventually had another ring made with the diamond from this ring and one my mother had given me with a similar diamond and wore it on my right hand. This was symbolic of my mother and husband, both of my deceased loved ones, and brought me comfort, though it did not help me answer the larger questions I was grappling with.

# Why me?

When Steve died, I had already suffered two significant losses – my mother, the year before, and the ten-week-old fetus I miscarried a month before Steve passed. Why was all of this happening to me? I didn't have any answers, all I knew was that I seemed to be experiencing more than my fair share of tragedy. Other people noticed it too, hence the pity that hung like a cloud over every conversation. My sense was that my proximity sparked some fear of their own mortality and that of their loved ones. They simply couldn't imagine coping with so much death.

For a while, I thought about moving away; that could have been easier. But where would I go? Cheyenne was an option, but my father wasn't much help and there wasn't anyone else there to help me. I also wasn't sure what kind of job I would get there. I could move somewhere new, but then I would be even more alone. In the end I decided to make a more incremental change; I used the life insurance money to purchase a house. It was nice to have some more space and comforting to take the stuff that hadn't fit in the apartment out of storage. This move, while not as drastic as a change of city, was nevertheless a sign that I was ready to take my next step. In less than a year I had experienced the death of a spouse and two major moves and it was exhausting just to think about it. I was so grateful to have Steve's family to support me in all those challenges. They were the light in the darkness of my day. But they couldn't be there all the time. I had to spend most of my time alone as a single mom.

As the year anniversary of Steve's death came around, I decided that it was time to take a sabbatical from work. I was incredibly stressed out and not really engaged with my clients anymore. The economy had also crumbled, and though my clients were fairly stable, I was nowhere near hitting the benchmarks I had in the past, nor was I motivated to do so. Earlier in the year, I had decided to go back to school and was accepted to a Master of Organizational Leadership program. Now, after going through my finances, I realized I had enough money to take a year off work and focus on school fulltime. Plus, I needed some time to really grieve and deal with my new reality. I had worked through the first level of grief, meaning I was able to function day to day and had survived the holidays, but I had barely scratched the surface of my pain. Working all day and caring for Chase at night just didn't give me the time that I needed to process all the questions and issues that kept coming up and figure out what I needed to do in order to heal. And I just wanted time to cry. Alone. In my bed. For a whole day.

When I submitted my resignation, my company said that they would consider rehiring me if I decided to come back. This was comforting; it is never easy to walk away from a job, especially in a recession, so it was good to know I had a potential future opportunity. In the meantime, I needed to figure out what I wanted to do. Fortunately, I was able to afford daycare, which allowed me some time alone to process my future.

Free time. It sounds great in theory, but shifting gears is not so easy when you're used to running around from morning till night. That first day after dropping him off, I returned home, sat on the couch and found myself instantly bored. I laid down on the couch to take a nap and quickly realized this is not my style. Reading had always seemed to help, so I scanned the bookshelf and came across "Overcoming Life's Disappointments" by Harold S. Kushner. I started flipping through it and there, page fifty-three, I saw the following line in italics:

*What happens to you, no matter how hurtful or unfair, is ultimately less important than what you do about what happens to you.*

This sentence stopped me in my tracks. I read it again, and again and had that, *Yes. This is it* feeling. And in that moment, a deep shift occurred. It allowed me to consider the possibility that this situation didn't have to define me as "that woman that was widowed at a young age." It could, however, inform my life and how I live it, and that I actually had a choice about that. This happened to me. I didn't have a choice in the matter. But I didn't want to live like an old hermit. I wanted love! I wanted more kids, for Chase as much as myself. I wanted to have fun and travel. I wanted to be successful in business. Yet how could I move on from this darkness to a future that seemed so far away? I had been thinking I might want to start my own business? Would that be possible? It seemed daunting, but I had just experienced one of the worst things that could ever happen to a person, and I had survived. I had strength and courage inside of me, and if I could handle this, perhaps I could handle other challenges as well.

I decided to take a road trip to figure things out. I had friends in Arizona and California I would love to see, and I owed my father a visit as well. The more I thought about it, the more excited I became about getting out on the open road. The plan was to drive to Cheyenne and stay there for the month of July. At the end of the month we would visit the spot where we'd spread Steve's ashes, then my dad would drive with me to Phoenix before flying home. I would continue to Las Vegas and Los Angeles. My ultimate goal was to come back to Minnesota with some clarity on whether I truly wanted to start a business. This was a start! Something I could look forward to, something I could focus on, something that was moving my future forward.

I found some friends to watch my cats for the two months I was going to be gone and arranged for my dad to fly to town. We would drive to Cheyenne together. As the trip got underway, I felt a sense of freedom that I hadn't felt in a long time. There was travel planned, adventure, new sights and experiences; this was going to be a much-needed break from reality!

Of course, it's impossible to completely escape. The trip started out with Chase screaming that he did not want to go – not the best place to start. Eventually he got settled and the thirteen-hour drive to Cheyenne was uneventful. It wasn't until we got there that I started to realize things were not so great with my dad.

Dad was a retired veterinarian. He had owned his own small animal practice in Cheyenne for thirty years. He was a kindhearted man who rarely said words that weren't kind and thoughtful. He was quiet, though, and preferred being alone to groups of people. He had grown up on a ranch in Lander, Wyoming and had the classic cowboy persona – quiet, with a very deep soul.

Now I started noticing a change in him. He was able to carry on a conversation just fine, but there were little things about his behavior that were just a bit *off*. Things like driving fifty-five miles an hour on a eighty-mile-per hour road or leaving the garage door open when he went out with Chase. I also noticed a highway patrolman's business card in his bathroom. I didn't know what these things meant, but intuitively I decided that I was not going to let him drive on the trip to Arizona. It would be a couple more years before I found out that what I was witnessing was the beginning of an aggressive dementia called Lewy Body Dementia. Back then, though I didn't want to admit it at the time, I knew his future was dimming.

We had a nice time visiting Arches National Park in Utah, The Mittens in Monument Valley, and Canyon de Chelly National Monument in Arizona. We then headed to Sedona after a colleague of mine had told me it is a good place for people who are mourning. I thought that maybe my father could get something out of it too.

As we arrived, I could feel that there was something different about this place. We didn't have much time there, as my father needed to be in Phoenix the next day for his flight home. I hadn't researched the place, so after checking into our hotel we decided to take a walk downtown and explore. There are a lot of shops with crystals and psychics and lots of interesting things, but neither my father nor my two-and-a-half-year-old were having any of it! One of the shops offered a crystal healing and psychic reading, but when I asked my dad if he wanted one, he looked at me like I was crazy. He did agree to watch Chase while I had one, so we went back to the hotel and went swimming for a while, hoping that would make Chase sleepy, then I left the two of them with a DVD player, and videos.

I was extremely nervous as I headed back into town. I had never had a psychic reading, and I was hoping that maybe I would hear from my mom and Steve or get some insight into this journey I was taking to figure out the rest of my life. I almost backed out when I got to the store. What if people think I'm crazy to do this? It was such a silly thought, but the nerves were definitely there. I didn't know how it worked, so I just walked in and let them know I was there for a reading. People were milling around the store, and nobody seemed to pay any attention to me when I said that, almost like it was normal. That made me feel better. I relaxed a bit more when the women came to get me. I wasn't sure what I was expecting, but she seemed normal enough too. She took me to a room in the back of the store that had a regular table and a massage table in it. There were different rocks and crystals all over the room. She had about five sets of cards on the table - a set of playing cards and some other sets of tarot or oracle type cards. She asked me to pick out a set for her to read. I knew what tarot cards and oracle cards were, but I was a little scared of them, so I chose playing cards. They seemed safer for some reason, without all the crazy pictures. I wasn't sure how she was going to "read" playing cards, but I was open to it. She shuffled the deck, then asked me to pick out cards. Once I had done that, she set them on the table and studied them for a while. She asked me if there was anything in particular that I was looking to get insight about. I told her that my husband and mother had passed and that I was on a road trip for clarification of my future. She studied the cards again, then said that she uses the cards and her intuition to provide the reading. She said that she was also a medium. She said that Steve and my mother were very proud of me. That they both thought I was doing well with my son and that they loved me. She said the cards said that I would start a business that was going to be successful after a lot of hard work. She said that I had some talent with writing and that could be something I pursue in my future. She said my mother was sorry that she couldn't be there in physical form when I had my baby, but that she was there with me. She said that they were both with us while we were on our journey. She said that my mother was worried about my father, that he wasn't feeling well but wasn't telling anybody of his symptoms. She said that Chase is a light. I had to ask her what that meant, because I had never heard that before. She said that he is there to brighten up the world and that people are attracted to him and that I needed to help him keep that. She said that people that come here as a light are so bright that people will follow them, but it can be very hard to maintain.

She then had me lay down on a table and did a massage with different crystals. The massage part was good, but I wasn't so sure about the crystals. I didn't understand that part. The reading was nice, though. I felt as though I had connected with my Mom and Steve! And they thought that I was doing well with Chase! It was so strange for me to think about them being in heaven and "watching over me." What did that really mean? Did they watch me go to the bathroom? Did they care? Did I care? Were they judging me, and were there areas in which they thought I was falling short? Did they agree with my decision to keep Chase in daycare even though I wasn't working? How can they "help" me?

After Steve passed that was what people would say – "Now you have angels in heaven that can help you from afar"; "Chase's dad will always be with him even though he is in heaven"; and so on… Those were nice sentiments, but what did they really mean? How would he be with us? I felt this woman had connected with him and my mother, but I was still so confused about how it worked. They may very well be there, but I couldn't

41

see them or feel them. I couldn't hear them either. The only connection I had noticed up until this point was the malfunctioning phone line and the feather at my feet at lunch that day.

As I left the store to head back to the hotel, I did find a feather on the sidewalk. Must have been a coincidence! But what if it wasn't? What if it was a sign from my mother and Steve? What if they were telling me that it actually was them? I still couldn't wrap my head around it, so I just decided to allow it to just be.

I walked into the hotel room to find a crying Chase and a frustrated and slightly scared-looking father. Clearly, things had not gone well. Dad couldn't figure out how to work the DVD player or the TV and he didn't know how to entertain a toddler. The latter was not that surprising as Dad was rarely around little kids, but how could he not know how to work the DVD player or the TV? I was puzzled and more than a little concerned, but I simply did not have the wherewithal to deal with it at that moment. I had faced too much already.

After an uneventful evening we headed to Phoenix, which was a sweltering one hundred twenty degrees. Quite a shock to the system after a relatively comfortable Sedona. Once my father was safely on the plane to Wyoming, I enjoyed a nice visit with my friend in Phoenix, then headed to Steve's brother's in Las Vegas and finally to my friend's house in San Clemente, California.

By that time, I had been on the road for about a month. We had seen some great sites and visited some great friends, but I hadn't quite figured out what I wanted to do with the rest of my life yet. I had some long discussions with my friends in California about the options. Should I start my own company? If not, where did I want to work? What was the point of it all?

These questions were still lingering in my mind when one day I was driving on Interstate 5 near Aliso Viejo in Orange County. I was one in a sea of millions on a twelve-lane highway; traffic was stop and go so I had a lot of time to think about what I was doing. What was I doing in California at that moment? Why was I there? My friends were nice to let me stay with them, but it was a bit of a burden and I still felt like I hadn't come to any conclusions about what I was going to do next. Then, a thought occurred to me. What if I start a business and it fails? The next thought I had was that I had been through a lot in the last year, more than most women in their thirties. Then it hit me. What I had been through was probably worse than a business failing, so who cared if it fails? That was it! That was the answer! I had already been through tough times and I have survived! I could survive the challenges of entrepreneurship! It was an epiphany. It was a moment of clarity. It was something to hold on to. A glimmer of a future that was starting to be created. Could I do this as a single mother? Chase's uncle watched him a couple of nights a week, so that was helpful. I still had a non-compete that had a year and a half left on it. I had enough money to live for two years and finish my master's program. I could use what I was learning in school to help me create a business plan and prepare me for my new path! This was it!

A month of traveling, getting out of Minnesota and having some new experiences had helped me get to this point of clarification. I felt so much relief. Finally, I had something to look forward to and work toward. I wanted Chase to see me as someone that took what happened to her and figured out a new path. I wanted to be an inspiration for him and I wanted him to see me as someone who was successful, and who didn't give up. Someone he could look up to. Suddenly I had a whole new energy about my life; a purpose beyond survival for the first time since Steve had passed. It was still a little scary to think about, but I felt it was better than it being in a black hole.

For the last leg of my trip, I met my dad at the airport in Newport Beach and we headed up the coast, first to San Francisco, then the Sequoias. From there we visited a friend in Lake Tahoe and then headed east and made it home in two days of straight driving. Chase was a champ the whole time except for one moment in Fargo, North Dakota when he let us know that he was definitely done with being in the car.

Once I got home, I immediately got to work, investigating the Staffing Industry conferences that were out there. There was one in Las Vegas in October, and I booked a ticket so I could start finding vendors and people that could help me. The next couple of months I spent putting together a business plan. I found a template online that was easy to use and pursued the classes in my master's program that would suit my plan. I wanted my company to be based on integrity and ethics, so I had an Ethics and Leadership class; I needed to understand how to manage the financials, so I signed up for an Accounting and Finance class and a Strategic Finance class. To help me with marketing there was a Strategic Marketing class. To help me with my business plan there was an Entrepreneurship class. There was also a Strategic Management class and a couple of others that would be helpful! I felt more excited than I had in a long time about what my future held.

# Dating Again

It was October 2010, about a year and a half since Steve passed away. I had taken my ring off at some point earlier that year, and during my road trip I had even started thinking about dating again, or least thinking about thinking about it. As always, the question of, *Am I ready?* was at the forefront. I also wondered what others, and Steve – if he were in fact "watching" - would think. I knew I wanted to have more children, and since I wasn't getting any younger, I knew the time was coming when I would have to seriously consider getting out there and start dating again.

When I returned home from my road trip I "accidentally" found Wayne Dyer's book "The Power of Intention." I can't exactly remember how I came upon this book, but it has been a powerful teacher in my life. There is a section that talks about how the Universe needs to know what you want so that it can get it to you, so it helps if you make a list. At the time, I didn't really believe that, but thought it was an interesting concept. I decided that I would make a list of my perfect boyfriend and see if it would actually happen. I threw in some characteristics that were pretty simple, such as good with Chase, kind, fun to be around, nice to me. But then I got bored and decided to make it hard for the Universe to find this person. It was kind of a dare to see if this thing really works. So, I put that he had to be romantic and that he had to be Australian. Ha! Let the Universe deliver on all those things, I thought, then I kind of chuckled to myself that this was dumb and put it away.

At the end of October, I dropped Chase off at Steve's cousin's house and headed to Las Vegas for the annual conference of the American Staffing Association. I was excited to take this next step. There would be seminars to take and a big expo to attend. I met with vendors and people from all over the country, several of whom had staffing firms similar to the one I envisioned. They gave me valuable information about what they would have done differently if they had to start again; for example, three people told me that if they could go back they would do it alone, rather than with a partner. My excitement grew when I connected with a company that could help me finance my business when I started it and a company that could help me with insurance.

On the third day of my five-day trip, after the happy hour and dinner, I was walking back to my hotel on the Strip when I saw a mime on the sidewalk. I would have walked right past him but to my surprise he spoke to me. Then someone behind me said something to the mime, and I heard the distinct ring of an Australian accent. I looked over at him and asked him where he was from. Originally Perth, Australia, he said, but he was living in the States now. I told him I had spent a year in Hobart, Tasmania while in college and before I knew it, we were walking up the Strip together. His name was "John," and he lived in Los Angeles. I told him about my time in Tasmania, and he told me what it was like for him working in Canada and living in the United States. We went into the Irish Casino on the Strip and started walking around that, and then found a seat and just kept talking. We talked about EVERYTHING!

It was like a scene in some romantic movie where two characters randomly meet, talk all night, and realize they're in love by the time the sun comes up. Well, not quite the love part, but we had so much in common it was like there was a powerful, magnetic pull between us. We talked about what he was doing here, and how his parents were visiting from Perth and were traveling around the U.S. and had decided to stop over in Las Vegas because it was a favorite destination for Australians. He had sent them to bed and decided to just take a walk on the Strip to see what was going on. I told him about being a widow and that I had a son that was almost three years old. We talked, and talked, and talked until about two in the morning, when I finally told him that I had to go to bed because I had to be at the conference early. Before we parted ways, John asked if he could take me to the magic show with his parents the next evening. I happily accepted, and he said he would text me to let me know where and when to meet.

I woke up a few hours later and knew there was no way that I could get to the first session of the conference. I needed to get some more sleep. But how could I sleep when I had met the Australian that I had put on my intention list? What!? Was this possible? He was charming, sweet, a gentleman, not dating anybody, and I was going to meet his PARENTS this evening. I was excited, nervous and scared all in one. Everything told me that I should definitely go to the magic show that evening. What would it hurt to go? Then I thought, what if he didn't text me? All of these emotions were running through me and I felt like a schoolgirl who's thinking about kissing a boy for the first time. I hadn't felt that way in a really long time, and it was a very welcome change from the pain and suffering that I had experienced in the last year and a half.

I finally got up and headed to the Staffing Association meetings, but I was checking my phone every five minutes to see whether he had texted. I told myself it was no big deal if he didn't, but it WAS a big deal. This was the guy! The guy that I had put down on my list, or at least he seemed to be so far. Finally, in the middle of the day, I got a text from him about where to meet and what time. Wow, this was crazy. Really? Am I going to do this? What if his parents were weird? What if it was weird to meet them? I had just met him last night, wasn't that beyond bizarre? On the other hand, he seemed normal, and intuitively I felt like it was all going to be good. I decided to go and see what happened.

My feeling turned out to be accurate; John's parents were incredibly sweet and nice, and I could tell they were genuinely happy to meet me. The magic show was great, and I laughed more than I had in a very long time. After saying goodbye to his parents, John and I decided to explore Vegas. We walked for what seemed like hours, and the conversation flowed just as easily as it had the night before. John talked about growing up in Perth and what had made him decide to move, first to Canada, then the United States. He talked about how expensive L.A. was and how he lived in the back of a gym because he didn't have enough money for an apartment. He also told me that he'd been a Taekwondo champion back in Australia and might have made it to the Olympics if not for an injury. He was picking himself up from that and doing some website work on the side. I spoke more about Steve and Chase, and that I was here to learn how to start a staffing agency. I wouldn't exactly say we fell "in love" that evening, but we were certainly interested in seeing where this budding relationship would lead. At the end of the evening, John asked if he could take me to the airport in the morning, as

I had a noon flight back to Minnesota. We weren't sure what the next step was, but we were going to talk about it in the morning.

All night, I couldn't stop thinking about it. How could I randomly meet someone on the street who had so many characteristics from my list? John was sweet and romantic and Australian. I couldn't believe it. It was beyond my expectations!

The next morning, as we were sitting in the airport terminal together, John told me he had a wild idea. He was driving his parents around the United States and their next stop could be Minnesota! It would take them a couple of days to get there, then they would stay for three or four days before his parents headed back home.

I told him I thought it sounded great, a little crazy, but great. Then he gave me a long, hard kiss - one of those kisses you know you'll never forget. And here I was still buzzed from meeting the man of my dreams on a Las Vegas street! I couldn't wrap my mind around that, let alone that in a couple of days he would arrive on my doorstep in Minnesota, with his parents in tow! I got on the plane in a state of pure joy and anticipation of what was to come. When I got home, I found a feather in my driveway. I wasn't sure what it meant, but it seemed like a positive sign.

John called me several times from the road. I knew the late autumn Minnesota weather would be quite chilly for these folks from Australia, but they didn't seem too worried about it. In fact, his parents seemed excited to spend some time in Middle America, with an American; they were even interested in seeing one of the Great Lakes! I on the other hand was starting to get nervous, not only about spending more time with John, but about introducing him to Chase. Would it affect my son to meet a guy I was romantically interested in? After some careful consideration I decided that Chase was old enough to enjoy meeting a new man in his life and young enough that he wouldn't remember John if he never saw him again. But what if I did see him again? I told myself he was just coming to visit, that it wouldn't necessarily become anything more, but what if it did? Was I ready for that? And, was I ready for "that"? Intimacy with another man? What would Steve think? I didn't think he would want me to be alone. But what about his family? Was a year and a half enough time for them to see me with someone else? I knew I would have to cross that bridge when I came to it, whether with John or someone else. My thoughts then circled back to John. Was this a good idea? Finally, I decided the worst that could happen was that we didn't get along and then he would be on his way. Once I realized that, I gave myself permission to be excited.

They arrived in St. Paul three days later and checked into a hotel close to my house. We all met for dinner and John and his parents met Chase for the first time. They fell instantly in love with him. This was no surprise - Chase was a cute blonde with a cherubic smile, a sweet disposition, and an enduring personality, so pretty much anyone who met him fell in love with him. When I asked what they wanted to do while in Minnesota, they had their list ready: see Lake Superior, go to a big box warehouse store like Costco, and go shopping at the Mall of America, not necessarily in that order.

We had an amazing few days. I took them up to Duluth, where we went to museums and sat and watched the water. We went to Costco, and they were in awe of the number of products and the size of products that you could get there. And like most people, the Mall of America both overwhelmed and delighted them. In the process they learned more about how the average

Americans live than they did while visiting the tourist spots in California.

John and I didn't get a lot of time to hang out one on one, so I was thrilled when after his parents flew home, he asked if he could stay for another couple of days. We spent the next five days getting to know each other; each morning I would drop Chase off at daycare then pick John up at his hotel. We returned to the Mall of America and played games in the amusement park; we went to a couple of movies and sat in coffee shops and talked for hours. The time went all too soon, and by the end of it he was asking if he could come back and when. I told him that he was welcome whenever he wanted. A couple of weeks, he replied, and just like that my life was changed in an instant. All of a sudden, I had someone in my life that was fun and interesting. Someone who liked me and adored me. I wasn't sure if this would be the "one", but I was open to finding out!

When John returned to Minnesota, I set up a dinner with my friends, so they could meet him. It was a bit awkward – one, because it was five women and one guy, and two, because it was like a question and answer session. Later, I learned that they were all less than impressed by him; he didn't have a college education, and the web business he was running was really nothing to write home about. None of that bothered me, though; I was just looking for an Australian that was romantic, and he fit that bill!

John stayed with me on and off for the next six months. We spent Thanksgiving with my friends in Colorado. Steve's family graciously invited him to their house for Christmas and it was the first time he had seen snow and gone ice skating. Though I was sure Steve's family was struggling to see me and Chase with someone else, they showed no signs of it. They were nothing but kind and welcoming to John. Just after New Year's I got a wedding invitation from a friend in Tasmania; he was getting married that April. It was perfect, I thought. I hadn't been back to Australia since college and now was my chance to visit friends and bring Chase. If John came with me, I could introduce him to everyone and then we could go to Perth and visit his parents.

I was surprised to find that John was far less enthused. Whenever I brought up the trip, he would change the subject or say it wasn't a good idea. I couldn't understand it. Why wouldn't he want to show me where he had come from, as I had him and his parents? And then it occurred to me. He didn't have a visa! He was in the US illegally! It all started to make sense. When I confronted him about it, he didn't admit to anything but said it would be hard for him to travel in and out of the country. I thought that sounded very fishy. After that, his behavior changed. He became demanding of my affection and controlling of my behavior. Clearly, he hadn't picked up on the fact that I'm an independent woman who does not like people telling me what to do. Finally, one day I told him I didn't think it was going to work out between us. Though we'd had a great time together, I wasn't willing to sacrifice my integrity. I couldn't be around someone who felt like it was okay to be here illegally, and I also refused to be controlled.

John's departure was bittersweet; on the one hand I was sad to see John go, as we had had many good times together. On the other, I learned several things. First, I learned that making a list worked for me! How exciting! A list! It worked! Second, I realized that my list needed to be WAY more detailed than just a few bullet points. So, I said goodbye to my Australian boyfriend grateful for a fun experiment that had given me some confidence in myself and allowed me to feel good about finding someone that could be in my life long term.

A couple months later, Steve's grandmother passed away. I was out of town when I got the sad news. She was a fun lady that wasn't afraid to tell you her thoughts and she was beloved by her family. That night I had a dream where she told me that I needed to start dating again. It was an odd dream, but the timing was interesting, so I decided to think about it. The next morning, I found a dime on my bathroom counter that was not there the night before, so I saw that as a sign that I needed to do something. I saw an ad that day for E-Harmony and decided to sign up. This was rather odd, as I had always thought online dating was silly, but I decided to go on the site anyway. It looked fairly safe but seemed like a lot of work.

Shortly after looking at the website I found another dime on the floor of my house. I didn't think much of it until I took Chase to bed that night and saw another dime on the floor of the stairway. It was odd to see that many dimes! Someone in Steve's family had told me earlier that day about finding dimes and believing it was their grandmother that just passed. So, although I had been skeptical of signs since Steve's passing, I got the feeling that these dimes were his grandmother's way of giving me the thumbs-up about online dating. I also knew I wasn't going to be going out to the bars and I had no idea how else I would meet anyone. That same night I began the lengthy process of signing up. I had to fill out a whole personality profile, then answer additional questions about my various likes and dislikes and preferences. At first, I had no idea what my preferences were. They were asking things like "What time do you go to bed and wake up in the morning?"; "What is your relationship to money - spend, save, or both"; and "What types of movies do you like?" A lot of questions that to me seemed to have little significance in determining compatibility. Does it really matter when someone wakes up in the morning? At first it seemed overwhelming and pointless, but I kept going, more out of curiosity than anything else.

Next, I had to fill out my profile page. What in the world, I thought, do I write here? There were many blogs and sample profiles to use as guidance, but I had no idea how to describe myself to potential suitors. It was all too much, so I stopped for a couple of weeks, then picked it up again when I felt inspired. Remembering the success of my list, I decided to write down all the aspects that I was looking for in someone, then put myself in that person's shoes to describe myself. This was what my list looked like:

- Kind
- Fun to be around
- Needs to be okay with my independence (I made sure to put this one in!)
- Must not be allergic to cats (not an option)
- Likes to travel
- Likes to read books
- Likes coffee and wine
- Wants to spend time together
- Likes to go camping
- Healthy lifestyle – takes care of himself

As these were my interests, listing them made it much easier to write my own profile. I included a couple of photos of myself that I thought were decent and then hit complete before I could chicken out. It was a little scary, yet at the same time the idea that finding someone from the comfort of my living room was appealing.

The system quickly sent me ten guys for which I was a possible match. I began perusing their photos and profiles and found several of them quite interesting, to say the least. There were a lot of guys in action shots; one guy was on his bicycle and another mid-workout at the gym. Some of them had kept their kids in the photo but whited out the ex-wife. Many guys had a beer in their hands, which I thought was a turnoff. In the end, I decided to send a note to half of them.

In responding to a potential match, I had a list of questions, similar to the initial ones I had answered, from which to choose from. These included, "How do you spend money? A. Spend it B. Save it C. Save a little, spend a little"; and, "If you were taken by your date to a party where you didn't know anyone, how would you respond? A. Stay close to my date, letting him/her introduce me. B. Find a spot at the back bar alone, letting them work the room. C. Strike out on my own, introducing myself, and making new friends."

It was kind of like passing notes in class. And this was just the beginning. Once I had my answer, then what? I had to figure out if this was really what I was looking for in a partner. Some people didn't even respond to me. What did that mean? Ugh, this was all a lot to sort out. I was committed, though, so I continued the process.

Among my exchanges, there was one guy, "Harry," who stood out. After a week or two I finally gave him my email address. He was very deep and contemplative, which was new for me. I found I liked it, and after several rather deep conversations about life, I thought it might be time for us to speak in person. We arranged to meet up for coffee at a restaurant by the river. This was the first official "date" I had been on in years, the last one being during the four years Steve and I were broken up. I was nervous but excited as I walked into the restaurant and joined him in a booth. He had bright blue eyes and a warm smile. He was a bit older than me, but he had a presence about him that was attractive. The conversation began with the usual formalities, including what we did for a living. Harry was a graphic artist and had worked for some big advertising agencies downtown but was currently freelancing. I told him I was working on starting a staffing business, then we moved onto more personal topics, some of which we had already gotten into over the computer. I talked about being a widow, and he told me he wasn't dating anyone and hadn't been for a while. He also talked about his daughter and I told him all about Chase. We really hit it off, and the whole time I was thinking, *this guy seems to fit everything on my list. How is this possible?!*

As we were walking out to the car, Harry asked if we could meet again, then and gave me a soft kiss. Gentle, sweet, affectionate, and perfect. I drove home that night walking on the moon. I couldn't believe that for the second time I had found someone who hit all my boxes! He was smart, driven from what I could tell, he loved family, he was fun-funny, and we could have those deep, almost philosophical conversations I had come to enjoy. My belief in the write-down-what-you-want-and-it-will-come-to-you power of intention was growing stronger.

After that first date we continued our email correspondence and made plans for dinner at Minnehaha Falls. A series of lovely dinners and get-togethers followed. One night while Chase was with his cousins Harry came over for dinner. We had a great time preparing the meal together and talked and into the wee hours of the morning. He invited me up to meet his parents, who lived on a lake in northern Minnesota. We had a lot of fun with them. And so it went! He met Chase, I met his daughter, and we started dating seriously. Harry seemed to adore everything about me, from my thoughts on life to my super high heels with glitter on them. He made me feel beautiful and interesting. He was also supportive of my starting my own company and used his expertise as a graphic artist to help me design my logo and letterhead; he even found me someone to help design my website. Everything seemed perfect until, little by little, the truth of his situation started to rear its ugly head.

Harry had never married his daughter's mother, and I knew early on that they did not get along. As time went, she became more and more of an issue in our relationship. He would spend hours talking about how much he hated her and everything he was doing to get custody of his daughter. I remember one occasion when he spent the entire day composing an email that he was going to send to her. Then it occurred to me, why wasn't he working or looking for a job? It wasn't about money - he told me his parents, who were quite wealthy, were supporting him - but his lack of gumption. Here I was, burning the candle at both ends between school and working on setting up my company, and I was dating someone in his mid-forties who seemed to have no drive at all. There was also the one non-negotiable on my list that he did not have: a lack of interest in travelling.

In the end, however, it was his behavior toward me that forced me to call it quits. About a year into the relationship, he started to become verbally abusive, telling me things that I needed to fix or work on or how much I sucked at this or that. He was telling me these things, he claimed, for my benefit. Of course, I knew better, and I knew I didn't want that in my life;

I certainly didn't want Chase to be around someone like that. It saddened me when I broke off the relationship, because even though I really did like him my gut was telling me this guy was not the one.

Harry seemed to accept my decision when he came over and collected his things from my house. But about a week later, he decided to come to Chase's daycare and sit in the parking lot until I arrived. It got more disturbing from there. He followed me from the parking lot to a restaurant where I was having dinner with a friend and her daughter. I did not see him in the parking lot or notice that he had followed me at the time. After we ordered, a member of the restaurant staff came to the table and said they were concerned about someone outside who was staring at our table and pacing back and forth. My friend and I both said we knew no one who would do such a thing – It never occurred to me that it might be Harry! The staff came back a couple of times to ask if we were sure and when we left, they followed us out to our cars to make sure we were safe. That's when I saw his car leave the parking lot. I couldn't believe it! He was stalking me! I called the police, who immediately talked to him. Thankfully, this scared him enough that he never did it again,

Though I was sad that another relationship had ended, I also felt that I had a much stronger idea about what I was looking for in someone. Over the past couple of years, I had continued to read the Outlander series and had fallen in love with the lead male character, James Fraser. In him, Diana Gabaldon had created the ideal male: a strong, proud warrior who was also sensitive and kind. Most importantly he adored his time-travelling wife, Claire, with total abandon and appreciation for her strong will and independence. Though he had dealt with a lot of adversity he had held onto his humanity and his enormous capacity for good. I decided that my new list included everything to do with James Fraser, including his red hair. Not because I love red hair, but because I still had some lingering skepticism about this list thing and needed irrefutable proof. And, based on the last relationship, I decided to add that the guy I met had to be financially secure and have a job and skillset that he could make a good income with; he also needed to see the value in traveling, not just a tolerance for it; and have no issues with a previous girlfriend/ spouse and no issues with children. He had to be emotionally healthy, with no capacity to stalk or harass someone. When I was done, I checked and rechecked the list several times and decided I was satisfied. This was it. The perfect list!

Looking back, I realized that when I first started dating (and for some time after that) I had no idea what I really wanted in a partner. I thought I just wanted a nice person who was romantic. Boy, I was wrong about that! I'd heard the saying that we don't learn with words, we learn through experiences, but only now did I fully understand the truth of that. How could I have known that what appeared to be "romantic" could sometimes really be "controlling"? Or that a seemingly normal, confident person may not actually be all that emotionally healthy or stable? Steve had never been controlling, and he was the picture of stability. Dealing with these sorts of people, while sometimes hurtful, had helped me further define what I was looking for in a person. And I was confident that person was going to come into my life. He had to, right, because I had the list!

I logged back into E-Harmony, and this time I was much more particular about who I was connecting with. I had my list and if they said something or acted on anything that was not aligned with it, they were out. I wasn't going to waste any more time! I now looked at it almost like a job interview. That may sound disconnected and just weird, but I knew what I wanted, and I was not going to settle! I went on way more coffee dates than I did before. I also vetted people much more thoroughly before going on that first date. That meant sending them more in-depth questions through E-harmony. One of the most helpful questions was "If there was one thing you would like your significant other to do with you every day, what would it be?" One guy had a picture of him on a racing bicycle, and when I asked him that question, he replied, "Ride bikes every day." Well, that eliminated him because riding bikes every day did not appeal to me. The next guy had a photo of himself in his fireman's bottoms with his shirt off. He had nice muscles. He said that he would want his girlfriend to work out with him. Nope, he was out. One man said that he was a sex therapist. He wanted to know if I was comfortable with that because most women he'd met on e-Harmony were not. Nope, I don't think so. There was some comfort in knowing that I could avoid wasting my time. If I had met any of those men in a bar, I wouldn't have had the opportunity to ask these questions in a detached, non-judgmental way. As I weeded through potential matches, I started to realize I was actually having fun. I felt confident that my list was going to work, and it was just a matter of time for the right guy to show up.

One guy made it through my vetting process with flying colors, but when we met in person, he told me all of the stories of all of the previous women he'd gone on dates with. I didn't mind this, because of the stories were quite interesting, but then he proceeded to tell me how smart he was and how he'd gone to Harvard for a year but couldn't take it so now he was working as a lab tech. He was all over the place, so he was out. Next, I had plans to meet a guy for dinner and he owned a small business in town, so I looked up his website. In the back of his website there was a whole page dedicated to his ex-wife and how much he hated her and what she was doing to him. I decided to cancel that dinner.

At one point there were two guys in the running. The first was "Fred", a small business owner with whom I'd had some great exchanges on the site, so I decided to go out with him. That date was a lot of fun! He was funny, charming, and down to earth. At the same time, I connected with another guy, "Chad", who seemed interesting, but I wasn't sure about how much he had traveled. This was a recent addition to my list of questions: Where have you traveled to? If they said the only place, they'd visited outside the US was Mexico, they were out because if you don't like travel you are not going to spend money and time going on trips. So, I sent Bachelor #2 a note asking where he had travelled to. Though he seemed a little put off by it, he wrote back and said that he had been to Germany, India, and Sweden. Now we were talking!

Chad and I made plans to meet at a bar close to my house. When I saw him drive up that night the first thought I had was Ugh, he's one of those. He was driving a pick-up, and while that in and of itself isn't bad, they are usually driven by a certain type of guy. The type that leaves their wives or girlfriends every weekend to go hunting or fishing. However, when I met him, I didn't sense that at all. We decided to sit outside on the patio under an umbrella. After about an hour it started raining and we decided to stay out there in the rain. The poor waitress had to keep running out in pouring rain to serve us! It was fun, and it showed me that he was willing to have a little adventure and wasn't going to let rain ruin his fun. I appreciated that. Before parting ways, we discussed getting together again. It turned out we both had trips scheduled and wouldn't be able to get together again for about a month or so.

Now I was in a bit of a dilemma. I liked two guys at one time, which was unchartered territory and a little uncomfortable. I decided I would play things by ear and as soon as one of them became more serious, I would end it with the other. I didn't want to hurt anyone's feelings, but I also knew that when you go into online dating, you assume certain risks. I decided to go on a second date with Fred the business owner. We went to a restaurant in St. Anthony Main, a hip neighborhood in Northeast Minneapolis. We took a walk by the river and had a lot of laughs. Then he started talking about his ex-wife, who he had been divorced from for a little less than a year. He shared his concerns with how she was handling everything and on and on. I was empathetic but concerned because I could tell he still had some grief around the situation. On the other hand, I also was aware that how he treated her through the divorce said a lot about who he was and what kind of partner he would be. He also had a giant meal with dessert. He was a big guy and that part didn't bother me, but something about it seemed really odd.

Not long after that, I set up a second date with Chad, the truck guy. I'm not sure why, but this time I noticed that he was dressed really sharp. I was still in my first impression stage and since I hadn't seen him in a while, my first thought that came to me was that he was probably a preppy rich kid and my mind went to the possibility that he was probably stuffy and rigid. I didn't notice that on the first date that we were on, but fun to be around was on my list and I wasn't all that interested in stuffy and rigid. We had a great conversation over dinner, but the part

I will remember forever is that after finishing his game hen, he proceeded to lick each one of his fingers. Once he did that, I figured he probably wasn't all that stuffy after all. Now I was in a bind, because I still liked both of them. It was time to go into research mode.

# Moving forward - Finding light in the darkness

I decided to do some online research on the two guys I was dating. I couldn't stand dating two people at once and I needed something to draw me to one or the other. When I typed Fred's full name into Google, I found his Facebook and Twitter pages. His Facebook page was private so no luck there, but I was able to access his Twitter page. The first thing that popped up was a photo he had posted. It was a photo of a very large sandwich and a comment that said something like, "I can't wait for this to get into my belly." Now, I have never minded bigger guys; there is something about a big guy wrapping his arms you that is like a cape of protection and warmth. On the other hand, if you are taking pictures of food and eating a lot of unhealthy foods and if you are already uncomfortably large, your health is probably not a priority. That may sound terrible, but health consciousness was on my list and I want to honor my list. So, it was one check mark against Fred.

I then moved on to Chad, but other than a private Facebook page I couldn't find anything online about him. If I wanted to find out more, I would have to go on another date. We went to nearby Stillwater and had a lovely dinner and a lot of laughs. I also had an opportunity to learn more about him and his life. Not wanting the night to end, we found a bar where there were people dancing. We found out we liked the same types of music and had a great time dancing the night away. Shortly after that date I decided to look at my list again and look at it specifically with Chad in mind.

- Kind - Check
- Fun to be around - Check
- Needs to be okay with my independence – Seems to be so far
- Must like cats (not an option) – My shy cat that stays away from strangers ran up to him when he walked in the door - Check
- Likes to travel - Check
- Likes to read books – I don't think so, unless they are about science or math
- Likes coffee and wine - Nope
- Wants to spend time together - Check
- Likes to go camping – Check
- Healthy lifestyle – takes care of himself – Check
- Financially secure with good job – Check
- No issues with previous girlfriend/spouse – Check
- No issues with children – Check
- Emotionally healthy, no capacity to stalk/harass someone – Check
- Scottish warrior – Hmmmm, not sure on this one. But he does have red hair like Jamie in the Outlander books.

He does seem to appreciate my independence like Jamie does for Claire and he has experienced a lot in his life like Jamie and has overcome it all with grace.

• Needs to be completely okay with spending time with Steve's family – Not sure yet but doesn't seem opposed to the idea of it.

The only two things Chad didn't have on my list were a love of reading and liking coffee and wine. I sat and looked at this list again, this time with Fred in mind. He didn't even come close. And the winner is…Chad! It was amazing how this list worked! He pretty much had everything I was looking for! I immediately sent an email to Fred and let him know that I was going to be exclusive with another guy because I didn't like dating two people at once. He was sweet and said he was disappointed but understood and respected my decision.

Other parts of my life were also falling into place, and quickly. My business plan was coming together and the end date for my non-compete was fast approaching. I had enlisted my brother-in-law and another friend to help me get the business started, but I had to complete my application and submit my business plan in order to get financing. Once that was secure, I had to lease a space and purchase furniture. At the same time, I was finishing up my master's degree, for which I had to complete a final project. In other words, I was busy! I felt like I had a purpose. My life had meaning again. I wanted to show Chase that I was not going to waste away in a joyless darkness because Steve had passed away. I wanted to show him that I was a survivor, that I could be a successful businesswoman and be an inspiration to him. I wanted him to have a fun childhood, one that wasn't sad because his father was gone, but one that was full of joy and fun and good memories. I knew that being a working mother would be a lot for me to handle, but I knew that my growth and development would only benefit his in the long run. I knew that I needed to work through my grief and sadness and understand death in a deeper way. What happens when we die? If I do find someone else, what does it mean to that new man that I am a widow? Is he going to understand my experience and respect it? Is he going to allow me to talk about Steve? Will he be okay hanging out with Steve's family? They are still a big part of my life and always would be. That was not negotiable. Would this man be able to be a "dad" to Chase? He needed a male influence, and though his uncle still took him one or two days a week and that was a huge help, it wasn't enough. Chase needed someone that could teach him about being a man and help him manage all his exuberant energy, which was something I was terrible at. I really didn't want to wrestle with him, I felt like I really didn't know how. I didn't want to hurt him! We wrestled a little bit, but I just wanted to hug him and love him, not hurt him. I didn't know how to explain going to the bathroom as a boy or any number of future questions he would have about becoming a man.

In the coming weeks and months Chad and I spent more and more time together. He finally met Chase on Labor Day weekend when we all went to the water park. At first, Chase wanted no part of Chad, and he really didn't like him holding my hand. As the day went on, however, they started enjoying each other's company. I realized Chad had a way with kids, he was one of those people that kids tend to like and want to hang out with. At one point I had to run to the car and asked Chad if he could watch Chase for a minute. Chase just looked up at him and said, "Come on, let's go" and dragged him into the large wave pool. They have been inseparable since that moment. The next time Chad came to our house, Chase wouldn't stop talking to him. They have a connection that is very special and very deep. The more and more I spent time with Chad, the more I realized that he fit my list and he even fit things that weren't on my list that should have been on my list. My heart was full. I had found someone that loved my son like his own, treated me like gold, and honored my independence. Is this okay? What would Steve think about this? What would his family think? What does this mean for my relationship with Steve now? I didn't want to dishonor him in any way. What happens when we die? Is he happy for me? Is he mad at me? I was not sure what to think. I knew that Chase needed me to be happy and move forward with my life, but I still wondered. I wanted to make sure that I honored Steve's memory and that Chase never forgot him. These thoughts still filled my mind even whenever I was with Chad. We got married about a year and a half after we first met, and Chad adopted Chase about a year after that. Chad has fully embraced Steve's family without any hesitation. We spend every other holiday with Steve's family, and Chad and Steve's dad take Chase on a fishing trip to Canada every summer. Our daughter Kayla was born about a year and a half after we got married. Steve's parents are Kayla's grandparents too; they have fully embraced her to be one of their family members.

# What Happens When We Die?

After Steve passed away, Chase would see him periodically. It would be random, like the time we were eating dinner after he came back from his grandparent's house. I asked him how it was, and he said he had seen his dad, Steve. When I asked him where he saw him, he replied, "We were playing outside, and he was standing by Grandpa." I then asked what he was doing, and he said, "He was there and then he was gone." Chase wasn't sad or happy about it, just matter of fact.

It had happened again at a Thanksgiving dinner with my friends in Colorado. Chase, who was just three at the time, told me he had seen his dad at the party. When I asked more questions, he wouldn't answer them, but as we were driving to the airport the next day, he asked where his dad and his grandma had gone. If I asked questions such as, "Did you see them?; What did they say?; What did they look like? and so on, but he would just ignore me. I never saw anything. I did have a dream once about my mom - we were going shopping and she looked happy - but that was about it. I remember reading many stories of people seeing their deceased loved ones after they had passed, usually around bedtime, and one of Steve's nephews (his sisters' son who was four at the time) said he saw Steve at the funeral standing behind his identical twin brother Scott as he spoke on stage. I didn't understand all of this. How can people "see" someone that has died? This was yet another step up from the feather signs it had taken me so long to accept. I looked in books and online, but I never really got an explanation that made any sense. I was talking to a colleague of mine one day that was open to this kind of thing and she gave me the name of a medium who also did house clearings. I called the woman and set up a time for her to come to my house. When she arrived, I remember thinking that I was going to pay all of this money to someone that is going to clear my house? What is she going to "clear"? What does that even mean? She had two rods in her hands which she used to move the energy. She told me they are called dowsing rods, the same kind of rods used to find water. It all still didn't make sense to me, but I trusted my colleague, so I was going to see what happened. As she was going around my house, she felt Steve in different places. This was great but confusing. How was he here, in different places? She had me tell him that it was okay for him to go, that I was okay now. She said that some of his energy was stuck here and I helped release it. She said that he was happy that I'd found Chad. Really? Now, that is cool! I had a lot of questions about what she was doing, I didn't understand it at all. She recommended the book "There's More to Life Than This: Healing Messages, Remarkable Stories, and Insight About the Other Side," by Theresa Caputo (aka the "Long Island Medium"). She said that Theresa explained it all in a way that was easy to understand. I had never watched her show, but I ordered the book online that day because it looked like it was exactly what I was looking for.

When the book arrived, I devoured it. It was such an eye-opener for me, especially after losing two loved ones. I suppose I never cared to understand it before, but now I needed to know.

She explains in that book how people that have passed give her signs and signals in order for her to do readings. She says that God is energy, our souls are made of energy, and how our energetic vibrations get stronger as our souls grow and as we ascend to higher levels of soul growth. She mentioned Albert Einstein saying that "Energy cannot be created or destroyed, it can only be changed from one form to another" and relates that to how our body and soul are both energy. The body is heavier energy and your soul is lighter, more purified energy. Theresa also says that we chose to go into a body because we learn more while in physical form because our bodies allow us to feel joy, happiness, laughter, the feeling of petting a dog, smelling a rose, kissing your partner, but also negativity, pain, sorrow, and loss, which are both positive and negative and are all lessons that allow our soul to grow. You can't do that without a physical body. She says that souls that have crossed over don't need a physical body to transfer their energy, they make her sense and feel things by transferring their thoughts, feelings, and messages to her. She says that we do this in physical form too, that our thought vibrations are powerful energy and we can use it to influence, attract, and manifest our ideas and desires. Our thoughts can help determine our success, outlook on life, and attract our circumstances in life. This was a new way of looking at life for me. As I was reading it, it made sense to me because how else was she getting messages from deceased loved ones? Messages that resonate with the person receiving it, almost every time, but through an energetic connection.

There was one section of the book that hit me particularly hard. Many people who have died have told her that there was nothing anybody could do to prevent their death and that their loved ones shouldn't feel guilty about it. She told a story of a boy that died by drowning and his parents were devastated. They kept wondering what would have happened if they wouldn't have gone to that pool. They came to her to do a reading and the boy told her that he was going to die, that it was part of the plan and if he hadn't died by drowning, he would have had to go in a different way that would have been even harder on the parents. When I read this part, I wondered if that was really true. Do we really have a day that we are going to die? It really bothered me because I previously learned and believed that we have free will, so if we have free will, then why is the date of our death predetermined? For me, this meant that Steve was going to die that day no matter what. That was the plan. So, if I hadn't married him, I wouldn't have to deal with this? Or would I have married someone else that would have died? Was this part of my plan, to have someone die so that I would have to learn all these lessons? This idea intrigued me, but it gave me so many more questions than answers.

Another section that really spoke to me was her description about what happens when you die. She says that she has been told by Spirit that when you die, your soul peacefully detaches from your body and you are greeted by your deceased loved ones and then you are guided to a brilliant light. Our guide that has been with us in spirit throughout life guides us through our journey in the physical world and we get to see how our actions affected others. We experience what we made others feel – pain, happiness, sadness, et cetera. and how that was related to our plan for this lifetime. She said that our purpose is to learn lessons to develop our soul over lifetimes. Lessons about patience, joy, faithfulness, selflessness, and so on. We are also here to help others learn lessons or make good on things we have done wrong. We choose our bodies and our families to help us accomplish our goals. Woah. What? We see how our actions affected others? We experience what we made others feel? That is deep! I remember after my mom and Steve passed away, especially after Steve passed away, I had a deep desire to understand what happens the moment we die. I saw my mother after she passed and was deeply disturbed because she wasn't in there. It wasn't her anymore. It was a little frightening because I really wanted to know where she went. Was she in the room with us? A couple of days after Steve passed away and everybody was at my house, I went in the backyard and was crying and was thinking, where are you? and I heard this voice say, "It's so amazing here, I wish you could see it. You would never believe it, it is crazy." The voice was so strong and clear that I thought I was imagining things, but was I? Was he in a place that I could communicate with him? I had put that out of my mind because it was still beyond the realm of possibilities to me, I was dealing with his death, he was gone, and I was in agony. After reading this part in Theresa's book, I thought that maybe I could hear him that day. But why couldn't I hear him now? Anytime that I wanted to? I asked him to come to me in dreams and that hadn't happened. Why was it so random? Why could I clearly hear him that day, but I haven't heard him since? When I was thinking about him did he know? Does he know everything about what I'm doing? Is he in the room with me when I'm kissing Chad? Does he know my thoughts about him? What about the negative thoughts? If he went through a life review, he must know some of the things that I felt about him when he was alive, some of the moments that weren't so great? If this is true, it completely changes my perspective on life. If everything that we do gets reviewed at the end of our lifetime then what we do better be in integrity because the other person is going to find out eventually. If it is not while they are alive, they will find out when they die. That is deep.

As I continued to read, I still had more questions: so, do you get mad and angry when you find all of that out in heaven? What about hell? What qualifies you to go there? Theresa says in her book that she has interpreted by Spirit that there are low levels of energy on the Other Side, but they have never used the word *Hell*. She feels that these individuals have a lot of work to do on the Other Side or by reincarnating until they get their lessons right to move up to higher levels. Spirit has told her that they can do their learning with a loving, forgiving God, not in a tortuous place. She talked about a story where she channeled a girl who was murdered by her best friend's ex-boyfriend. He killed her and then killed himself. The mom, dad, and two brothers were all there in the room when she was channeling her. She told Theresa that her brothers weren't going to like it, but she brought forward the soul of the boy who killed her. He apologized to her mom for his crime. The man's soul said, "I am sorry for taking your most precious gift." The brothers were upset that she was with him in heaven. Theresa said that she lowered her vibration to his level to bring his soul forward to give her mom healing. The mother was grieving her daughter's death but also was wanting to know if the man felt remorse in heaven for what he did. His soul went on to say that not only does he have to account for what he did, he has to endure the family's heartache over the life he took. The message also validated that the girl's soul hears her mom's thoughts. Wow, I thought, this is a whole new way to think about what "hell" could be.

# We still have issues even though you are dead?

Before experiencing so much loss, I probably didn't give much thought to conflict resolution. I probably thought that once someone dies, all your issues and challenges with them go with them, and you are free from it. Unfortunately, that is not the case. It's almost worse, in fact, because you can't work things out with them and ask why they were the way they were and why they did this and that because they are gone.

My mother and I had an okay relationship, but there were issues. There were a lot of things that I didn't like about her behavior towards me and towards other people in my family. It wasn't abusive or anything - she was a kind, loving woman - she just had some erratic ups and downs that affected all of us. Behavior that nobody that knew her would believe; it was all done privately when nobody else was around. I did try to talk to her about it, but she either didn't want to or did not have the capacity to deal with or understand what she was feeling or how it impacted us. In any event, she would not talk about it or admit that she had done anything wrong or upsetting to us. It did affect me, though, because I was so sensitive to it, and it did affect my feelings toward her. So, when she passed away, it was almost as if there was a wound that was left open and raw, something that was left unsaid or undone. At the time I felt like it would be with me forever, something that was heavy on my heart. I didn't like the feeling. Every time I tried to push it down and ignore it, it would persist, and it wouldn't go away. It was as if I somehow needed to deal with it, but she was gone so I didn't know how.

Then Steve passed away and again, he was a wonderful loving, kind-hearted man, but there were things that happened that we never resolved and feelings that I had toward some of his choices that I would now never be able to understand. These emotions were always there and underlying my journey of grief. I often wondered how I could get over them or resolve them. At the time I felt like a victim. A victim of their actions toward me, and at the time I felt as if I was stuck with them forever.

A couple of years after Steve passed away, a friend recommended a book called *Radical Forgiveness* by Colin C. Tipping. The book opened my mind to how my pain and heartache and my reactions and perceptions of my mother and Steve reflected something in me that I needed to heal. Whoa. Really? It was much easier to just be a victim and blame them, especially because they are gone, which made it even easier. But now that I had some awareness, I couldn't do that anymore. I also definitely didn't want to be considered a victim; even if this was all internal dialogue, I strongly feel that I am NOT going to be a victim. Tipping describes "victim consciousness" as the conviction that someone else has done something bad to you and as a direct result, they are responsible for the lack of peace and happiness in your life. Traditional forgiveness is when we are willing to forgive but we still have a need to condemn. Radical forgiveness has the desire to forgive and NOT condemn. The first step to heal these emotions according to Tipping is to shift my perspective that the behaviors they exhibited toward me were for my own healing, that they had done nothing wrong. They simply played a part in my drama acting in support of healing my own soul challenges. This is the radical part of forgiveness that he teaches, which is the fact that nothing wrong has happened.

I decided that I needed to figure out what these perceived wrongs were teaching me about myself so that I could heal. This path felt much better than simply blaming Steve or Mom. It also felt as if I would get some emotional relief from my pain with regard to my relationship with them. I decided to set up a day-long retreat with a spiritual mentor that I trusted to help me really dig back to those events that were holding me back. We spent the first half of the day going through all my memories and topics that were right on the top of my mind regarding my mother and Steve. Many of the stories or situations with my mother immediately revealed a theme, and that theme was that I often gave my mother my power. My mother had a very strong personality. Whenever we were around other families, she was often leading the group or the center of attention. This was my perception anyway. I am sensitive and intuitive and more of an introvert and I would say that I was probably the exact opposite of my mother. I am more of an observer, listener, and enjoy hearing everyone's stories and participating in them instead of being in the center of them. My mother didn't understand that. What my spiritual advisor pointed out to me is that my mother would say something to me and if whatever it was didn't "feel" right I wouldn't question her or say something to her because she was so powerful to me. She told me this happens a lot when we are young because she was my mother and I was supposed to believe and trust her. It is common that kids often take parents words over their own beliefs or feelings about situations, especially if parents don't ask kids to share their feelings and want to control how they feel. What that did to me as a child was to not "trust" what I was feeling, but trust what my mother was saying over what I was feeling. When I would feel that something wasn't right, I wouldn't speak up because I was taught that I needed to "trust" the adult. I would give my power away to that person and not trust my own guidance. Regarding my mother, I would invest in her beliefs and perceptions because I didn't want to disappoint her, but deep down those were not necessarily my beliefs and perceptions. In essence, I gave my power to her.

When I got older and had more of my voice, I would try to tell her my thoughts, but she didn't hear me. She wasn't interested in my voice at that point; she never was. My spiritual advisor helped me to understand that this wasn't my fault, this was her life challenge, not mine. She taught me that there were lessons in this for me. The main lesson was that I learned what it was like to have my power taken from me and to not have a voice. I didn't have to continue that, however. It was something that I could heal and learn to use in my relationships. She taught me that assertiveness means that you are aware of your feelings and opinions and that you state them to yourself and others in a way that respects other people's rights. An assertive person can be kind yet never should have to apologize for his or her feelings because feelings are to be honored and respected. She helped me work with Archangel Zadkiel who is the Archangel of forgiveness, mercy and benevolence to forgive my mother for taking my power and myself for giving my power away.

I wish I could say that I felt an instant healing after that session, but I'm not sure it works that way. I did feel better and had a better awareness of the feelings I was having toward my mom.

Sometimes situations would stir feelings or memories of her and I would do some meditations with Archangel Zadkiel about forgiveness and it would feel better, but I think that with our histories and lessons that we are here to learn there are always layers that need to be healed. I would say that I feel a thousand times better than I did when I started, but I'm still doing forgiveness work with my mother as memories still continue to bubble up over time. I am also learning to trust my guidance and my feelings and be true to those and not give away my power to people if they believe and think something different than I do.

I have also done some work on my relationship with Steve, which is much harder to talk about. I have found that when people die, everyone wants to think about them as a saint and not as a human being. People don't want to talk about the challenges you have had with them in life because maybe, as I did, they think that the problems go away when you die. But they don't. They sit there until you address them and heal them. Steve and I had a good relationship. We were in our twenties for most of our time together; we married when I was twenty-five and he was twenty-six, and he passed when he was thirty-three and I was thirty-one. Most of our relationship was when we were young and naive, not knowing much about life or having a deep understanding of marriage or relationships. I don't believe that Steve had been in a long-term relationship with anyone else, so there was no doubt that this was going to be a lot of learning for both of us one way or another. He came from a family of seven - three brothers and a sister - and two loving parents. He was raised half-Catholic and half-Lutheran in small town in central Minnesota. As I've mentioned several times throughout this book, Steve was the life of the party. It was his joy to make people laugh, and he had no problem making himself look silly to make people laugh or to get them to at least giggle. At his wake I had several people tell me that they had only met him once, but they felt that they knew him for life, that he was a friend for life. He had a close-knit group of friends that he grew up with and went to college with. It seemed that he was the glue of that group. He brought them together and forced them to have fun.

My best friends (all guys) from high school thought he was a "tool" the first time that they met him. He quickly used that to his advantage and made a funny joke about it that he brought up every time he saw them. I would say that they are still to this day sad to have lost him. At one point he made a t-shirt that he brought them to wear that said "dirtysdaman" on it. His nickname was Dirty, for two reasons: he did construction and often had dirt all over him, and he had a dirty mind. It was fitting.

When I watch Chip Gaines the star of Fixer Upper on HGTV, he really reminds me a lot of Steve. I think that as Chip did on one show, Steve would eat a Cockroach to make everyone laugh. He also had a heart of gold as Chip does. He was one of a kind, never to be replicated, even though he had an identical twin, they were physically identical, but their personalities were completely different. He was truly loved by all he met and a beloved friend to anybody who crossed his path.

Have you ever heard that people that are really funny are often depressed? Remember what a shock it was that Robin Williams committed suicide, because how could someone who brought so many people joy and laughs be depressed? I'm not sure how it works, but behind closed doors, Steve wasn't the same as he was when he was making everyone laugh at a party. Not that he was abusive or anything close to that, but he had a sadness about him that I would guess most people who knew him would be shocked to hear. I have a sense that because of his upbringing he was raised to give it his all, give his time, his energy, and his money if necessary, to people that needed him. Unfortunately, he never learned the opposite of giving, which is receiving. It's like yin and yang, the Chinese philosophy where opposite forces are complementary, interconnected, and interdependent; you can't have one without the other. If one is missing, there is imbalance, and that's when the problems arise.

Steve was a contractor for several years. He worked so hard and he absolutely loved his job, for it gave him the means to give people happiness in the form of something tangible. It was his joy to see their happiness in all his hard work. Receiving money for all that hard work, at a profit, was not as easy for him to manage.

My spiritual advisor and I worked through what I would consider typical relationship challenges when it comes to someone that loves to give but has a hard time receiving. I realized that in those situations I had no power to do anything, that I felt completely powerless when I would offer my love or my time or my energy and he couldn't receive it because he simply never learned how.

There was a time when he was having problems with his knee and he drove in extreme pain to the hospital and got signed in and was given a room and had a quick surgery before he called me. He didn't want me to worry about him. I rushed over to visit him, and he said he was okay and to go on home and sleep in our bed. I wanted to take care of him and to love him and dote on him, but he didn't want that. He didn't know how to receive my love and care and I felt powerless because I knew that was the truth. I know now that he did it out of his belief that he was giving me some freedom for the evening, but it was extremely painful and sad for me to experience that, because I couldn't use my desire to give him love and instead felt guilt and shame for not being there with him. His lesson to me was how important it was to not only give but to also receive someone's time, energy, and resources because it is an equal energy exchange. Going through this process with both my mother and Steve was life-changing for me. It allowed me to release negative energy that had been stuck within me and gave me more energy for personal growth and joy. It has allowed me to be more fully present with my family and move forward with greater understanding and awareness of who I am in this lifetime.

## Connection. Feeling Hope.
## Loved ones brought me here.
## Synchronicities, symbols, signs

C had and I got married in March of 2014 at the glass dome top of the Millennium Hotel in downtown Minneapolis. We thought March wouldn't be too bad weather-wise, but it was the coldest March in a century! The boiler in our hotel broke down that afternoon so the ceremony was quite cold, although it warmed up by dinner and the reception. Chase was excited to have a dad and was thrilled that "we" were getting married (we meant all three of us) and that he was a big part of the event. Our daughter Kayla was born in October of 2015 and then Chad officially adopted Chase in 2016. Chase took the last name Benning Swanson to honor both of his dads.

In the spring of 2016 I attended a retreat to have some time to myself after Kayla was born and give Chad and Chase some time with her one-on-one without me. The retreat was with a gifted spiritual leader and attended by ten women, half of whom had lost their husbands. It felt like a divinely inspired synchronistic group. We were all at different stages of grief at that point but still healing from our life-altering experience with death. There was a point during the weekend that we were all sitting through a guided meditation and during that meditation I finally connected with Steve! It was the first time since he passed about seven years before that I could actually see him. It started with him floating above my house. An angel came and I jumped on the angel's back and we started flying. He took me to the place in the mountains that we spread his ashes. It was as if he was acknowledging that he was there, and he knew what we did with them. It felt like he was happy with that location. Then he took me back to my house and we were in the living room and Chad was there with Chase and I was there, and Steve was there, and my mom was holding Kayla and we were all laughing and having fun together. He then took me to his parents' house. His whole family was there - his parents, and all his siblings and their families. Chad was there, too, as were Chase and Kayla and my parents. Just before I came out of the meditation, Steve and my mom and dad all came together and gave me a big hug.

The experience was so real, it's hard to not believe it really was Steve guiding me through it. I believe that I had healed enough that I was ready to finally see him, but also, I was in an environment that was safe and with a group of people who could support me as I connected with Steve in a divine moment. It was powerful because for me it was absolutely him, I now have no doubt that he is still around and that he was able to connect with me and take me on that journey. My heart was bursting. He showed me what had been in the back of my mind all along and that was whether he was okay with Chad? Was he okay that Chad was hanging out with his family? Did he know Kayla? Did my mom know Kayla? He showed me that all of those questions were yes, yes, yes, yes, and that it was all okay and it was all good. That he was with us during all of it and he was supporting it one hundred percent. I felt no jealousy or animosity from him, just absolute love for all of us.

I shared my experience with the group and it was touching for everybody, and it gave many of the other women in the group hope that they may someday also be able to connect in that way with their late husbands.

About an hour later, the room started getting really cold. We went to the hotel management and they said that the boiler broke down and they were starting it back up. Another hour went by and it was freezing in the room, so we asked for another spot and they found us a room in another part of the hotel that was warm. It occurred to me at that moment that the same thing happened on my wedding day with Chad. I told the woman leading the group and she said that it definitely could have been Steve coming to connect with me that shut down the boiler. She said that heaven is a very high vibration, similar to the vibration of love. Earth is a lower or denser vibration and it takes a lot of energy for our loved ones to come down and connect with us on our level. We must try to attain a higher vibration of love and joy for them to have an easier chance to make the connection. The energy of anger, resentment, fear, and hatred is way too dense for them to be able to wade through. Often when they come you will see TVs glitching or phone lines acting strange because Spirit is pure energy and because our technology uses energy to function. Maybe he was using the energy of the boiler to connect with me? I'm not sure how it all works, but I thought it was a very strange coincidence. He must have been at the wedding, bringing us his love and support and being present for all his family and friends that were there that day that were happy for me but still grieving his loss in some way.

A year later I went to the same retreat, hoping to connect with him again. I did, and this time it was as if he was right in front of me. He told me that he was sorry for some of the challenges in our relationship but that he worked hard to find me Chad (Wow!!!) and then he acknowledged that his sister Kim was having some health problems and he wanted to help her. At the end he said, "I want you to trust me," and then he was gone. This time he was talking to me! I had thought, based on Theresa Caputo's book, that mediums usually get symbols or signs when they communicate with deceased loved ones. That is not how this worked! It was as if he was right there in front of me and we were having a conversation. It wasn't quite a two-way conversation, partly because I was stunned into silence at the time. Later that afternoon the spiritual leader took the group into a bowling alley at the hotel. She wanted us to learn how to trust our intuition, so she blindfolded us as we were bowling. The first time I tried to bowl the ball shanked to the side immediately. She brought me over and asked if I had asked for help from Steve? No, I hadn't even thought about it! She said to ask and see what happens. I went back and pulled my blindfold down and asked him to help and then I heard him say, "I'm going to guide your hand." I didn't really try to do anything else other than pull my arm back and let go of the ball and I got a strike, all the pins went down. This was incredible! I was the only one that afternoon that got a strike while blindfolded. Was it him? I don't know, but it was a powerful experience for me. It taught me that he didn't interfere with my life unless I asked him to. And if I did ask, amazing things could happen! I had heard that before, and people always say that your angels and deceased loved ones are watching over you and that they are ready and waiting to help you, but they won't interfere unless you ask them to. It wasn't long after that experience that I started asking my angels and deceased loved ones for all the help that they could give me every day. I started meditating first thing each morning. When I begin my meditation, I ask for an MBO, a Most Beneficial Outcome of the day, and I ask for their help to make that happen. Why not?! If all I must do is ask and I can get the help of divine beings, I'm all for it!

# Appreciating life more
# than ever before

My father passed away in September 2017, ten years to the day after my mother passed and eight and a half years after Steve passed. Going through the experience of losing so many people in my life has been incredibly challenging, but in many ways, it has been a gift. I know that when I say that to people, they always look at me like I'm crazy. I think it is because they can't imagine losing their husband or family members. Or they think I am mean and that I wanted them to die, which of course is not what I mean. They simply have no reference point to death and the feeling of loss, partly because our society doesn't teach us how to handle it. These days, we try harder than ever to extend our lives. We eat healthier and exercise and are more proactive with our healthcare. Yet at the end of the day we cannot escape the truth: we all are going to die. All our loved ones are going to die too. Death is going to happen to everyone we love. I am grateful that I have had the opportunity to understand what that means more fully and clearly than most. I have also been blessed with other opportunities I probably wouldn't have considered had Steve not passed away. For one, I would probably never have started a business. I definitely wouldn't have written a book. I know that I had all of that inside of me, but I didn't know how to get it out, or at the time maybe I didn't have a reason to get it out. Why did it take a deep personal loss get me to really understand that life is short and that we could die at any moment and because of that I need to get on board with my purpose and use my gifts to help others? I'm not sure I have the answer to this, but I have seen this all around me too. People play small because they have no reason to play big. Why does it take something tragic to happen to us to decide to play big? To be bigger, to be better, to take risks, and to do more than we thought possible? To learn that fear holds us back from who we are and what we can accomplish? In his book, "Exponential Organizations," Salim Ismail describes a discovery that Google made about people in their company:

> "Google recently demonstrated that its best employees were not Ivy League students, but rather young people who had experienced a big loss in their lives and had been able to transform that experience into growth. According to Google, deep personal loss has resulted in employees who are more humble and open to listening and learning."

I wonder if it is because it makes us realize that we aren't on this planet forever. That we could be gone in a moment. We don't realize that until someone we love dies. It is almost as if we think we are immortal, or we trick ourselves into thinking that because we don't want to think about the other option which is that our time here is limited. We don't want to go there. Go to the possibility that we are going to die someday, that there will be a time that we are gone, and life will move on as it always did. Have you ever left a funeral and considered that a person's whole life was summed up in one hour or so? Once you leave, that is it. They are physically gone and there are people that will remember them, but they will no longer be present in that physical form creating anything new. What was said about them at the funeral? Were they remembered for their humor or their grumpiness? Are people saying poor so-and- so, they could have done so much more with their life, or are they celebrating their greatness? Does it even matter? What if we realized that we are only here for a short time, the date of departure unknown? That a funeral is only for the living, that we will be going to a place with no pain and no suffering? A place where there is no fear, anger, hatred, judgment, and pain. We will be in a place of pure positive love with the ability to reach through time and space and give signs to our loved ones who are still living. We will see the truth of our existence, that all of that fear and worry we had on earth was time and energy wasted, that there is an uncondi-tional love that surrounds us and supports us while we are here on earth, and that if we could only connect to that love, realize that no matter what, we are loved, we may be able to use that to pull us out of fear and into being something greater. Being the person that we came here to be, and to learn and grow, and become the best version of ourselves that we can be.

That is the path that I have chosen. Making the choice every day to fight fear, pain, and suffering, knowing that there is a greater purpose to this life and that this life is meant to be full of joy and well-being. That this life is meant to have its chal-lenges, that is how we learn, but we are not meant to stay in that place of suffering. The best part about it is that we get to choose how we show up every day. I could still be in a place of self-pity and suffering over Steve, my mom and my dad leaving this physical world. I now see it as they completed their time on earth and have moved on to greater things. I can still connect with them, even though I have no proof; I can't touch them, talk to them, or hear them. But I still get signs from them. I feel them in my life. I have experienced them whether in a dream or in a meditation. They still exist beyond this space and time. And they are not in pain or suffering! They are in peace, joy, and happiness! At my dad's funeral we played the song "Mountain Music" by the band Alabama. It was his favorite song and we would play it as we drove up the mountain to go camping. It has quite the beat and a fiddle section at the end that is fast paced. As I was sitting there, I felt and saw in my mind's eye Steve and my Mom and Dad dancing to the song. They were having fun. Everybody was sitting there in sadness and mourning, and I saw them dancing, laughing, and having fun. It was such a contrast that I felt like crying and laughing at the same time. My dad had shed his physical body, which was in a state of Lewy Body Dementia where his brain wasn't even functioning properly, and he couldn't get his body to move the way he wanted to, and was now dancing at his funeral. I didn't tell anybody what I saw, they would think I was crazy. But they were absolutely there. Recently, I went to the funeral of a woman that all three of them knew. And once again, Steve and my mom and dad were with her and they were all smiling. She was even laughing and tapping her foot to the music. For me, that was a reminder that we don't have to take everything so seriously. That we are not done when we leave here, but we just go to the next place, which seems and feels like a happy place, and that we don't take ourselves as seriously there. So why do we take ourselves so seriously here?

# What have I learned through this journey.

The last ten years have been a journey of the heart, one that has taken me from incredible sorrow to a path of joy. What started out as a journey to understand death turned into a journey about understanding life. Experiencing a deep personal loss transforms your life. Period. I have lost love and found love, only to realize that I never lost that first love to begin with because the love never died, it just changed form. I learned that it is possible to have a relationship again and still stay connected to my loved one that is deceased. How amazing that when people die, they are still present, even though we can't see them, touch them or talk to them, and we actually have the ability to connect with them if we choose to! We can get signs from them in many ways such as feathers, coins, birds, and butterflies, but also through devices attached to electricity like TVs, phones and lights. When our loved ones die, they are pure positive energy without a physical body, that is where we come from and that is where we go back to. There is no fear, anger, pain, or suffering where we go to, that is only for us to experience here on earth and is one of the reasons why we come here. When we die, we have a life review that measures not our accomplishments but how we made people feel, our behaviors and choices toward others during our lifetime. The review always comes from a kind loving place because there is no suffering there. This has led me to shift my awareness of how I live my life and how I treat myself and others, because our time here is truly limited. We could be gone any second, without warning. We don't have control over that, but we do have control of how we live every second of every day. I have learned that as I have started to understand all of these things, my grief for the loss of my parents and my husband has subsided and I can think about them and talk about them without becoming weepy every time. My memories are strong, and the love lives on, and I can connect with them any time I want to, if I choose to, and they are there like a beacon in the night supporting me until I see them again.

## In Loving Memory

This book is about my journey of loss and grief and finding joy, but I wanted to make sure that the reader understands that Steve was a valued friend, brother, cousin and uncle and a very important person in many of his friends' and family members' lives. I asked his friends and family to write their thoughts about what Steve meant to them and how they are working through their grief in losing him. The following are short essays from the people that were ready and willing to share.

Steve was always the life of the party with his brothers Mike, Scott, Troy, and their sister, Kimberly. Steve seemed to lead the group in pulling pranks and all sorts of jokes on people. When in high school and college all four of my sons worked on our construction projects and Kim waited tables. I found out later that she also would have liked to work construction, but it wasn't really acceptable for women to do so at the time.

I remember one prank Steve puled on my partner, Lyle. We were shingling the new homes we were building, and Lyle explained to Scott, Steve's identical twin brother, the proper way to apply the shingles. About an hour later, Steve was shingling on the other side of the house and Lyle saw that he was not applying the shingles in the proper way. Lyle went to him and said, "I just told you four houses ago how to do this. Why aren't you doing it the way I said?" and Steve answered, "You never told me, that was Scott" (even though he had told him before). Lyle just shook his head and then explained it to Steve again. These things were always happening when they were working for Lyle and me until those guys graduated from college and Steve started his own business. Then I would get calls from him while he was remodeling a house with questions as he was on the jobsite. I loved helping him out and seeing him and my other son Mike, who worked with Steve more often. I had retired from my construction business after thirty-six years, so I purchased an enclosed trailer to have my finishing tools handy in case they needed me. This would allow me to travel wherever his jobsites were and I could spend some time with them as they worked together. We always had good laughs every day, there was always something to giggle about.

On an April afternoon I got a devastating phone call that Steve had died that afternoon. I was at my daughter Kimberly's in Albert Lee, Minnesota. My wife JoAnn was four and a half hours away. We both needed to get to Minneapolis - one from two hours from the north and the other from two hours from the south. It was like my legs were taken from under me. I had nothing to stand on and no one close to catch me.

I realized that my life had changed forever. At the same time, I know that Steve's wife Wendy and son Chase's life had stopped, not just changed. I realized then that to help with my grieving I must help Wendy and Chase back to a normal family life. I didn't know how, but as a man of faith, I would be shown the way. One day I was looking at a cross and I thought if Mary and Joseph had to watch Jesus be beaten to death and not be able to do anything about it, I must do the same. I could not change what happened, but I could help my family, especially Wendy and Chase. Over the next five years that is truly what happened. Wendy found a wonderful husband and a wonderful dad for Chase.

Through this experience, I have been able to help other family and friends with their losses, and so goes the circle of life. We have to turn our devastating losses into positive change for the good of all.

Love, David Benning

━━━◆◆◆◆◆◆━━━

## April 27, 2009 – Worst Day of My Life

I'm Steve's mom, and I will tell you a little of my story of losing my son. It was about 5:20 and I had just had my 5:00 break at work when I got a call from my son, Mike. I don't remember the exact words, but it went something like this – Mike – "Steve died while working in his garage" – Me – "Steve Beck?" (a family friend) – Mike – "No, our Steve" – Me – "I'll be there as fast as I can." Needless to say, I was in total shock. I had to go to the office and tell my supervisors then out the door I went. I hopped in the car and to the Cities I went. I remember I had to get gas and wondered how can go into that station and not break down? I said a prayer (which I did all the way to the Cities) and went into pay. It was like a knife going through me when they said, "Have a good day." I just lost my son! While driving to the Cities I saw a sign that said Heaven is just a phone call away and believe me I used it. Now, I'm a fixer person and all the way down there between my praying I thought if I hurry and get down there, I can fix this, because that is what moms do. But this couldn't be fixed.

When I arrived at his home, people were already starting to stop by. It all was like a nightmare that I kept wishing I could wake up from. When I got done talking and hugging my daughter-in-law, I went up to Chase, my grandson's room and I just wanted to hold him and hope some of the pain would go away. As the night went on, more and more friends and family came. You sit and listen to all the stories (the stories helped a lot) but all you think of all the time is WHY? The first night I didn't sleep, the second maybe a few hours and that happened for a few weeks.

As a mother, it is so hard sitting down with your family and trying to plan a funeral, it all doesn't seem real. Now that I look back there were many ways God was walking with me through all of this. First, Pastor Tim was a friend of Steve's and I knew he was hurting also; he was so wonderful and understanding to us all. Then we knew the funeral home would never hold all the people for the service, so it just happens that Roseville

Lutheran Church was open that Saturday. I had gone to that church before and really liked it and it felt really welcoming. When we met with a lady there to plan the lunch and there again when I said we don't know how many people would be there for lunch she said, "Don't worry, I have never run out yet" (and she didn't). Another extremely hard thing for me to do was to go to the funeral home and say goodbye to my son. He looked so peaceful. He looked like he was sleeping. As I was walking out, they asked me to please take his bag of clothes; that is when I really lost it.

When the day came for the wake and the funeral, I look back and know God was carrying me because I couldn't have gotten through it on my own. So many friends and family, so much love from them all.

When I had to go back to work the next week, I wondered how I can possibly go in there. So, I said as I was driving there, "Jesus, you must take one hand and Steve the other," and I felt like they were there by my side supporting me. One thing I know as I look back on all of this sadness is that you are NEVER alone because night and day I knew Jesus was carrying me. Thank you, Lord Jesus, because without you, I couldn't have made it.

A message to my son – Son, I will be coming home soon, please be there in heaven to give me a hug and greet me.

All my love - Mom

———◉———

## Steve and Grief – by MB

There are only so many people that you interact with in life that really leave a lasting impression; Steve was one of those people. If I were to compare him to an object, it would be a Swiss army knife, because of the versatility that he had to utilize his dynamic personality to fit into any situation.

His sense of humor is the thing I miss the most. Here is a story that sums him up well. His mother in law had a surgery for cancer, they had to remove half of her liver. Before Wendy left to see her, he showed me a picture that he took for her to give her mother. It was a picture of himself lying in bed wearing nothing but a baseball cap and silk boxers (an inside joke between him and Cheryl). In those silk boxers he positioned a sixteen-ounce pop bottle so that it looked like he was fully aroused. You might be wondering why he would send a photo like that to his mother-in-law? Well, it was because he knew it was exactly what she needed at that moment in time. It was so ridiculous it was funny. It ended up making her laugh hysterically, even though that was painful, and for a moment it likely took her mind off what she was going through.

Steve was funny, charismatic, and outgoing. He loved to say things that other people were thinking but were too afraid to say. He had a huge heart and cared more about others than himself. He was someone that could be counted on in any situation. He has left behind a huge void that can never be filled.

Dealing with grief sucks, but if you don't deal with it, it will deal with you whether you like it or not. When you lose someone close to you, especially if it is unexpected, the raw emotion that you will likely be feeling will be unbearable at times. There will be some really bad days; try not to let them turn into really bad weeks or months. It's how you handle those daily emotions that will help you get through this process.

You will have moments when you are doing something and will be reminded of them, such as: hearing their favorite song or walking by someone and smelling the same perfume or cologne that they wore. This usually releases a flood of emotions. Whatever is stirred up in that moment - feel it. It's okay to laugh, it's okay to cry, and it's okay to be pissed. Just don't try to bury the emotions because they will come back at a later time and the next time that they do come back it will be ten times as intense.

One of the keys to dealing with grief is finding a process that works for you. It might help to tell stories about the person, it might work to reflect on some past experiences that you had with them, or it might be another person that helps you through it. For me it was the latter.

I spent a lot of time together with his one-year-old son that first year and the years going forward. I know that being around him was therapeutic for me and maybe in some way it was for him as well.

One very valuable lesson that I learned during that process is that grief doesn't strike everyone at the same time; especially really young children. For the first couple of years when I would pick him up from daycare some kid would say, "Chase, your dad is here," to which he would reply, "He's not my dad, my dad is dead." At that point he really didn't comprehend what that meant. It wasn't until he was about three years old or so that he started to realize what it meant to not have a dad.

There were times when he would just start crying in the backseat of the car and I would ask him what was wrong. He would say that he missed his dad. I would just let him air out whatever was on his mind. From that experience, I feel that it is very important to get young children talking about their feelings as soon as possible. If it is too uncomfortable for you to deal with at that time, try to find someone that you can trust to speak with them. Kids are curious, and they will have a lot of questions as they try to get a grasp on what they are feeling.

You might hear that dealing with grief gets easier with time. That might be true for some people, but it isn't necessarily true for everyone. One thing that will likely happen for most people is that the intensity of the emotions will subside over time. Based on experience, that will happen more quickly if you deal with your emotions in real-time.

In closing, don't let grief deal with you, instead, take it head-on and deal with it first.

---

## Steve – by Troy Benning

April 27, 2009, the day I lost my brother, felt like my breath was taken from my lungs. I remember the phone call from my other brother and dropping my phone. I'm not sure how long it was before I picked it back up but when I did, I could hear my brother crying on the other end and knew that what he said was true. I felt that I was in a nightmare, but I wasn't asleep. I was awake, it was real, even though it still didn't feel that way. That day was a haze because at the time I lived 1,238 miles away from my family in Las Vegas. I made plans for a flight and then missed that flight. All my friends from Vegas heard what had happened and got together at our favorite bar to offer support and keep me company. They helped me book another flight and stayed with me until I left. I'm not sure how I would have handled it if not for their support. The crazy thing was that I didn't realize that I was even feeling anything until my plane landed. I was numb after getting the initial news but when I landed back in Minnesota it was like hearing the news for the first time.

Seeing my family gave me comfort but also pulled at my heart because yet again I was reminded that what had happened was real. I noticed that my family and Steve's friends were in a different place emotionally than I was. We all had questions such as, what happened? What was he thinking? Did he suffer? Was he in pain? Who found him? Why did this happen to Wendy and Chase? To Steve? To us? You get your answers, but they are hollow. They don't fill any holes at that time. When I didn't get the answers I wanted, the loss and grief hit me like a linebacker hitting a defenseless receiver going across the middle of a football field. In that analogy it is only physical pain, but with death it seems like it is both emotional and physical. The bigger or closer the loss is to you the more you will feel both emotional and physical pain. How do you get through it? How do you move forward and move on? I don't know but I think you must move on with life, because I believe that if you don't you are disrespecting the memories of those who have left us. You have their memories and it is up to you to carry them with you. This can be hard because they can carry you down also, when they should lift you up! The memories and stories are your strength, your stop gap from making a major backslide into depression. I'm not sure if everyone who grieves goes through depression, but I know I did. As much as my family and friends helped, it was my memories and other stories about my brother Steve that truly brought me back and got me through. That was an amazing part about the wake. The day of the wake I was at the point that I couldn't cry anymore because I was walking around numb, but I got up enough strength to be there for everyone who came to pay their respects. Then everyone that came was crying and hugging us and telling stories about Steve which was so helpful for me to get through that day. But then there were some people that would say, "God Has A Plan " and I would get so mad because his plan sucks! I can't believe that His real plan was to have Steve die at thirty-four, leaving his wife and baby son. They would say, "Everything happens for a reason." Okay, great, so then you must know what that reason is?! They would say, "He is in a better place." I totally disagree and I'm very sure he would rather be alive and tucking his son into bed at night and kissing his wife goodnight and good morning! If where he is, is a better place then why are we so unhappy about it? If it's so better, then let's all go there! They would say, "I know what you're going through." Nope, because this is different for everyone and someone could have lost a friend and it could impact them way more than what I was going though. I believe some acceptable ones are, "Death f*cking sucks!!!!"; "I'm sorry for your loss, we are here for you"; "I have no idea what you're going through"; "I don't know what to say"; "He/she is going to be missed"; and in the right situations, "They were way too young to leave us"; and "No parent should have to watch their child die or lose their child." I really did not get mad at the people who said these things because in their hearts they meant well. However, when you have just lost someone, these comments can really get under your skin after a while of standing there hearing them.

I think the biggest step in my grieving process came while I was at my lowest point in my life. I was still living in Vegas and drenched in stress; it was weighing on me like a trench coat soaked and covered in wet concrete. I didn't know which way was up, I was drinking way too much and sleeping way too little with too many decisions to make, hopefully ones that didn't cause myself or others pain. With shortness of breath, chest pains, and lack of sleep I started feeling like a heart attack was right around the corner and I needed my brother who was also my friend and my sounding board to talk to. I decided to write him a letter that he would never read. The letter went something like this:

*Dirty, I don't know what to do. I think I have an answer but it's scary and will hurt so many people and change so many lives. I have no clue if that change although painful and big will be for the better or for the worse. Can I abandon people I love if I think it's the only way to save myself? Missing you and my family doesn't help. I'm raising someone else's kids that I love as my own but missing out on helping and seeing the only piece you of that you left behind grow. I think I'm in a relationship that I want and need but it has become so one-sided and mean-spirited. If you were here, you would tell me what you think! You would advise me on what to do. And whether I agreed or not I know it would help me make my decisions. I'm not going to get into detail about everything that's is going because I believe you're here trying to help. You know the thoughts about the relationship that are in my heart and head. You have seen what I am going through daily. And as I sit here with tears running down my face finding it hard to breathe, I find I feel again like I did when you died and am overwhelmed with thoughts of you and feeling pain I never truly dealt with or faced when you died. And now as I'm writing, my thoughts and emotions shift. As I am overcome by the grief of missing you....missing our talks, missing your sarcasm, that infectious smile, your laugh, your love for life, your love for people all around you, your love for those that you did not know, those people that you didn't call strangers but just friends you hadn't met yet. I'm sad for those memories we can't make. But on the days of celebration, I have a moment where I miss you and wish you are here but realize you would want us to just enjoy the day! Even if we would want so much more to be with you physically here, not just in spirit. Sometimes I miss you when I am with your identical twin brother Scott even though you two look so different to me, I search his face to see how you would have aged. I miss the memories that I had of us that I'm starting to lose, I miss the stories I loved and are now starting to fade from my memories. You can write them down and that helps, but they are so much better when they are still fresh in your mind. I will have one pop in randomly and know it's you saying hello. I see the truck you used to drive and burst into tears and it's just a truck and not your truck and I'm not even sure it that truck meant anything to you...but it still hits me. I think of you when new music and movies come out and think, Dirty would have liked that one...I don't dance as much as I used to when you were here which makes me sad. I think of something almost every day that I would like to tell you, but when you were here I didn't and now I wonder why...I miss my sounding board, my friend, my big brother, and the way you listened and would shoot me a straight answer. I truly miss that now that you are gone. I miss it with all my heart. It's such a little organ but man it can be filled with emotions. Thanks for listening I think I have my answer. As hard as it is to get my head around. I need to find someone here to fill the roll you played in my life. I'm not sure I can or want to, but it needs to happen. We will still have our talks, brother of mine, but I need someone who can answer after they listen. I miss you every day but more so tonight. I will hold you in my heart. When I get back to Minnesota, I will give Chase a hug from you and read him a book and tuck him in and whisper, "Your daddy loves you little guy more than you'll ever know!" And when he reminds me of you, I will take time and smile let him know that he is acting just like you did! Dirty, thank you for listening and giving me great advice one last time. Your right, it is a hard decision now, but it will make all the difference later. Please send me positive thoughts and love.*

There are many times in my life since that letter when I have had a conversation or sent thoughts to my brother and that letter was a big moment in my life for dealing with my grief. But I think I only got there because it was tied up with another stressful and emotional time in my life. I still to this day feel that I'm dealing with the loss and grief of my brother's death and the deaths of others in my life. His was just the most impactful. If you believe in the stages of grief and loss and that works for you, that's great. For me, I would say I grieve often, a little, sometimes, and when happy not at all. However, I never grieve without hope, for myself, my family, and my friends. I'm going to close with this today: I sit here with only pictures and memories left behind. I hate that we celebrate holidays, weddings, and family events without you. But take solace in the fact we all loved and cared enough to live life and take advantage of those moments while you were here and do our best to carry you with us since you left. I miss you when I see the things your son Chase accomplishes but I carry you with, I miss you as we all watch him grow but I carry you with, I missed you when I asked Kacey to be my wife and she said yes, but I carried you with. I missed you when we told our families we were pregnant, but I carried you with, I missed you when I announced we are having a boy, but I carried you with. I missed you when our baby boy arrived, and we gave him his name Keenum David Lee Benning, but I carried you with. I know in my heart there were times you were there, and I felt your energy with me, but just in case, please know Steve, my big brother, I did then and will always carry you with me. I like to turn on a song we both liked or watch a movie that we would quote word for word. Sometimes I pour a drink and wallow in it for a while and then realize that's not what he would want and pull myself back out and join the world and try to put a smile on someone's face like Dirty would have, because that is a far better way to honor his memory! Just realize none of it stops you just adjust your life and keep living laughing and spreading love to those around you, I find that is the best remedy.

---

## What Steve meant to us....
## By Scott and Lannette Benning

**What Steve meant to Scott:**

As twins, growing up there was always closeness and mutual understanding. Because we were identical twins, Steve was someone that I shared a connection with that allowed us to understand each other without needing to explain our individual actions, words, thoughts, or feelings. We could look at each other and know what the other was thinking. We could finish each other's sentences, even when we were away from each other for long periods of time. He was truly a close friend by my side for my whole life, no matter what came our way. It is a closeness that I can only explain as similar to a very committed spouse that you have been with for many years and know everything about them. And I mean everything, with no condemnation, just love. It is a deep familiarity around each other's thoughts, feelings and actions in every phase of life and any given circumstance. He was a safe place to be real and vulnerable, a secure place to exist. He was always my friend, even in moments of not getting along very well; I knew he was there unconditionally. This is how he treated others in his life, but this especially stood out in intimate and more personal settings. He would shine his light and soul, which was always authentic, and very hard to find in this world. This is what made him so attractive to such a diverse group of people. He was always open to getting close to others, as long as they were authentic, honest, trustworthy, caring, and humble. He was very gifted and a blessing on many levels. I feel extremely blessed that my soul mate, Lannette, and my two boys, were able to grab more of that before his passing.

**What Steve meant to Lannette:**

I had to do a little proving to Steve when I met him, while my eyes and heart were heavily focused on Scott. I thought this might be something he wanted me to respect, and since we all gradually spent more time together, on nights out, playing pool and darts, I believe he realized there was a loving, healthy future for me and his twin brother. We enjoyed many nights out with Steve and college friends, and many were closer than family at times. Steve, to me, was the brother I always wanted, yet never had. It's hard to explain, but because Steve was Scott's identical twin, I had thought we might possibly have a lot of similarities, as each having been Scott's other "half", so to speak. At the very least, it seemed to me, we were alike in many ways. Of course, our lives were on completely unique paths. Yet, I could tell we both had the same passion for wanting to help others shine, and we both had a flare for creativity as well as spontaneity. Steve accomplished this, extremely well, by illuminating his wild and witty persona that connected with everyone on some kind of level. I really couldn't believe how much I had laughed around him and how I enjoyed so much time around him and the people who appreciated him so, and with Scott as well. The two of them, together, visiting and entertaining, as well as the way they could play off each other, was priceless. Steve and Wendy moved to California for a while and when they returned to Minnesota, all the while leading up to his passing, he came by often and spent time with our family. He had worked on our property and nearby friends' properties, which allowed him to spend a little extra time with his nephews Cole and Caden. And it allowed each one of us the chance to bond a little bit with him when he brought his new son Chase. Steve was a good father. There were many, many years, five years in fact, where we missed our connection on this level. And Scott and I were really looking forward to growing that time with him and Wendy. I also thought Wendy, was like Scott, in many wonderful ways, too. The four of us had inadvertently compared our lives, shared stories, and realized many of the same curiosities in life. It was effortless, when it was just us. And this was an absolute blessing. And while Steve and Wendy just started their own family, connecting us all on that parent level, putting us on a similar life trajectory, it was at this time, I hold the closest, and remember as though it was yesterday.

⸺◦●◦⸺

## Things changed drastically after Steve passed...the grief process...

### Lannette's grieving process:

For several years, it was a huge process to address the reality Steve was gone. Our family had lost a future with him. One that was bright, that we just started to share with him and Wendy and all our boys. It soon became apparent it would be a unique challenge for all of us. Scott could look in a mirror and see his brother at times. He had this option his whole life, so this was familiar. For the rest of us, though, that familiarity, on occasion, had been heartwarming, but also heart-wrenching. I personally had been challenged with reluctantly having seen Steve during a family viewing to say goodbye after he passed, then having to see Scott sleeping, making me recall that moment time and time again. I had previously struggled with periods of isolation, with anxiety and depression, but having an occasional familiarity of Steve, knowing he was gone, was unchartered and unfathomable. No one seemed to understand or had even thought to ask me, how I was doing, except for Scott, my boys, and a few of our closest friends. I felt this uncharacteristic sense that I couldn't talk about my own grief. Many people simply presumed Scott, was inflicted with the kind of grief one might read in a twin study. They'd ask me how Scott was doing, but not I, nor Cole and Caden, and I'd respond truthfully, the best I could. Scott wanted it known that he was okay and found peace with Steve's passing, and no one could understand it. In hindsight, maybe they were just searching for that same peace through him. But I didn't understand it, nor had peace, either. It was all frustrating and confusing for me. And it became a further challenge for my family, for fears of potential accidents in our home, that might lead to harm, would sweep through me with no apparent warning or pre-thought. I had so many reminders and seen so many personality traits of Steve that were similar with my boys. I had to make sure everyone would stay safe. Maybe it was a distraction, at the least, since I was not finding resolution with my grief. I also carried a deep grief for Wendy, and my mother and father-in-law, and made my best effort to find extra time regularly with Chase, while he played with Cole and Caden. I did feel a sort of anguish, which was unjustified I know, for having been the wife of the other twin that was survived. It all became a bigger issue than one might expect from a loved one's passing, and events that played out became quite surreal to me. There was never a real way for me to heal with all the ongoing comments and people's change of behavior around us. Scott was soon getting upset with others, while for me and our boys, a simple gesture from Scott that was reminiscent of Steve, could capture a memory, provide a moment of tears, then open a healing family discussion. It really helped me, and our boys. This wasn't the case around others. No one could open up about their apparent grief. If they had, maybe gatherings could have been more healing for all of us. As for me and our boys, we continued to have more and more moments of peace, getting our thoughts off our chests, and in Steve's honor, those moments were filled with jokes and laughter. It will be ten years next spring, and knowing Steve is gone is still difficult. But he would want us all to move on. Scott and I will be celebrating our twentieth ʰ wedding anniversary in May as well. And though it's important for others, every spring we choose simply not to commemorate the day Steve died, but celebrate the days he was alive. To me, Steve was kind, funny, thoughtful, intricate, and involved. He was a kindred brother to me, as well as my husband's identical twin brother. He was the Godfather of my youngest son, a second Dad and Uncle to both my boys, and an important piece of my life and the life of my husband, Scott. He simply left us all too soon. Our time with him was cut short, and because Steve appears occasionally in our dreams, we believe is an absolute blessing for Scott and our family. This God-given connection, and turtles of course due to a dream, is how he continues to let our family know that he's happy, and that he follows the love of his life, Wendy and his boy Chase, along with their fun-loving new additions, Chad and Kayla. It is truly a gift.

## Scott's grieving process:

Steve's death put an extreme strain on my whole family and changed us all forever. As a twin brother, there are moments simply gone. No more picking up the phone at certain times of the year during annual events or other random times where we would connect for special moments. No more shared birthdays, no more bonding on parenting, no more very close friend, no more connection, and no more life co-journey.

Then there was the challenge of grieving friends and family, especially ones that were particularly close to Steve and Wendy. During gatherings, it was immediately apparent they would long for those moments with Steve through me. Both Lannette and I had great empathy for them of course but left many moments with the projection of memories or thoughts of Steve embedded upon me. Shortly to follow, as they focused their attention right through me, there would be some requests for me to offer impressions of Steve. I would oblige, happy that I was able to do it, but it was hard as I felt like it separated me from the moment. This whole process strained our family and made us want to pull back as we felt like we were bringing them all more confusion and more pain. Lannette and I even discussed acting like him as soon as we arrived at certain places in an effort to satisfy this need and allow us to just be ourselves for the rest of the time. Especially since those moments were left hanging, no healing benefit came from the impressions. Many of these moments had lasted long after Steve was gone, however, the way it became possible for me to get through the grieving earlier than most, and move on with this life, was having my faith in a loving God. As I prayed and listened, he blessed me and guided me. He gave me the right words I was looking for in the eulogy I gave for Steve. Typically, I don't remember many dreams, but he blessed me by having Steve come to me in a dream where I was able to say good-bye to him and we each were able to tell the other that we love them. This was very important to bring me closure, since our last conversation while he was living, was not a positive one. All of this helped me to strengthen my faith and allowed me to heal faster. I know that Steve's passing was not the end, just the end here on earth. I knew that he would feel and respond the same as me if the situation was switched. It doesn't mean that I don't miss him, that it didn't crush my family and me, or that it didn't change each of our paths forever leaving us with many "what-ifs". It means that I could find comfort and be at peace with it. None of us are built to carry such great stress, worry, or pain. We need to give that to someone that can carry it for us. When I did that, I gave it to Jesus, it changed everything.

I could live in the positive memories and avoid wallowing in the deep sadness and suffering of it all. We needed to get our lives, with our own challenges, back on track and not be set back by a date of a horrible life-changing event. Steve was a great big incredible chapter of our life, but now we have more chapters to write with him guiding us differently than when he was here.

———✦———

My name is Todd. I knew Steve Benning. I was born three months and five days after Steve in a town of seven hundred souls in central Minnesota. We lived five blocks from each other and played at each other's houses all the time. We went to Catholic school, junior high, and high school together. We Played football, basketball, and baseball together. We went to Hamline University and were roommates for most of our time there. So, yeah, I knew him. That is a lot of togetherness.

Steve was always the guy in the group who was up for anything. I tended to just be the guy with lots of ideas. Ideas that rarely went anywhere without Steve. He and I were a great team that way.

Todd, age nine: "Let's stay up all night and play Crossbows and Catapults."

Steve: "Sounds good. I'll set it up."

Todd, age seventeen: "Let's all just go to Hamline for College."

Steve: "I have the applications right here."

Todd, age nineteen: "This Hamline/St Kates dance is boring. Someone should go talk to that gorgeous blond in the red dress."

Steve: "Hey, beautiful. Let's Dance." (Yes Wendy, that was you.)

Todd, age twenty-three: "*Not safe to say in a book your children may get a hold of*"

Steve: "Already done, my boy."

Todd, age thirty: "Let's get in our best dresses and try on makeup."

Steve: "Um... NO!"

Okay, that last one did not happen, but it could have, and you get the idea.

Steve meant that I could be someone I never felt I was. I could be daring and outgoing and the life of the party, because he was always there to pick me up if I faltered. It is amazing how the people you meet at such a young age can turn into the ones you grow with.

Unfortunately, we lost Steve in April of 2009. When he died a part of me went with him. I miss my friend so much sometimes it hurts. However, as time goes on it gets easier to remember that he also left a part of himself in me. I admit I did not deal with my grief well in the first few months after he passed. I spent the time crying and wondering why this happened. Later, I realized I had already been doing things more like him and that he had rubbed off on me in ways I had not understood till then. Doing these things showed he would never truly be gone. I had been behaving slightly out of my comfort zone. I even emailed my future wife back when she emailed me to ask me if I wanted to go out. My inclination is to just ignore things that make me nervous. The old me, basically would have missed out on this whole life I have built. Thank you, Steve.

The final straw, the last clue, the piece de resistance, if I may, that shows Steve's influence is alive and well and that I am dealing with his loss with his own sense of humor and adventure, is in this very essay. When his wife asked me if I wanted to write this, Todd would have pretended he didn't get the message, or send an excuse about being too busy. However, in true Steve fashion, my response, "That sounds interesting. I would like to give it a try. You never know, it may be Pulitzer material."

I still miss my friend. I still want him around to do all the things we have missed these last years and the years to come. However, I know I'll see him when St. Peter opens those pearly gates and he is right there to greet me. I will get there. I know, because with all his influence, how could I not?

⟶ ◦◉◦ ⟵

## What Steve Benning Meant to Me

**9.23.18**

Where to begin? Describing what Steve meant to me is difficult to put on paper because of how special he was. Therefore, I will write it as only Steve would have appreciated, completely random. He was my best friend. He was friends with many people, but he could always give me advice that was from the heart and was spot on. It seemed to come to him with ease and clarity. A clarity, at times, I wish I had of myself. A clarity that I sorely miss in my moments of struggle with day-to-day life and I have not been able to replace since he left this world. He was the life of the party. Sometimes over the top, sometimes off the wall, but always fun. When we were just out of college, even though he had very little money, he would insist on buying everyone drinks when we went out. People would try to reciprocate, and he would deny them and say, "I want to hold it over your head." What? We loved watching football together and his favorite team was whatever team had Doug Flutie. "Flutie Flakes," Steve stated, several times on Sundays during Flutie's playing days. He loved him because he was the underdog that no one seemed to believe in but produced results at every level he played. I think Steve viewed himself as the underdog, a small-town person from Browerville who was going to make it big. We worked together at US Bank as mortgage consultants shortly after we graduated from college. We would take "executive lunches" to talk life and strategy on how we were going to create business. Steve would always push on thinking big and I was the "pragmatic" one bringing it back to what I perceived center to be. I loved how he thought about things with no limitations and envied his blue-sky visions, regardless of the topic. Generally, the conversations would shift to business we wanted to create, ideas we had and how we could run things better. It was energizing. His belief in positive outcomes was contagious. Steve and Wendy lived with Tanya and me when they had just moved back from California. I really enjoyed those days. Steve would claim he was an expert at grilling (debatable to false) and whip up some concoction on the grill for dinner while we talked life and sipped some wine or a beer. Somehow, whatever he made would turn out great. I remember feeling complete as a person at that time and it had a lot to do with how close we were to Steve and Wendy and how much I enjoyed coming home from work to spend time with them and Tanya. Steve was a giver, very in tune with those around him. We would take boys trips to Vegas frequently. Steve's giving made him a horrible gambler. He would "sprinkle" the table by giving money to random people at the table in an effort to bring good luck. It rarely worked out.

There have been many times where I have wondered if his positive nature would swing the other way in hard times and I just did not see it, or he did not communicate it. There are times where I wonder if I was as good of a friend to him and he was to me. Life was getting busier towards the end of his life as we both had kids; work continued to be busy and lived in opposite end suburbs of the Twin Cities, but we still remained close.

When I received the call that he had left this world, my world imploded. I had never dealt with a significant unexpected loss in my life until that moment. It was devastating. It left a hole in my life that I will not be able to replace. The grieving process is ongoing. I have buried myself into life with my family now that I have three kids and my work. I have some good friendships, but no one can replace Steve. His unique energy and fun-loving spirit are not replaceable. I wish we could have grown old together with our families fully connected. He would have been a great father, probably would have helped me be a better father, and I wish my kids could have known him. There are times when I speak to him when I am meditating, praying or simply thinking in the moment. I have felt his presence at times, especially when my mom was dying. I know he is present. I know I will meet him again when I leave this world, but I wish he was here working through life and bringing his light to it. I suspect the pain will actually grow as I get older and get more time to think about my life. For now, I am simply grateful that he came into my life and I was able to experience his friendship. He was truly one of a kind.

— Dan Ehler

## All About Steve By John Lorenzo

I first met Steve circa 2000 when he and his wife lived in California. He worked for a business partner of the insurance company I worked for. We had a joint presentation at a prospect late one afternoon and soon after, we decided to have dinner at the Claim Jumper.

During dinner, we learned a lot about each other. We talked about our backgrounds, our families and our goals. Although we were almost a generation apart, we had so much in common.

I believe we were both old souls and very traditional. We had great parents who instilled us with solid moral character and strong values. Over time, Steve and I became very close. We enjoyed teasing each other and bragging who was better at what sport and who was tougher, etc. All that being said, I really miss Steve. I really don't get close to many people and only had a select couple of real friends and confidants-Steve was one of them!

I could confide in Steve. I could ask him for advice and he would help me reason through the most difficult situations. He was a true friend who stood behind me and would never let me down. He was compassionate and classy. One example is when my father passed away. I was devastated. But who pulls up in his green car as I was talking to my neighbor—Steve. He had a sympathy card signed by his office and hand-delivered it to me. He drove a pretty good distance just to offer his condolences. That's the type of guy Steve was!

Steve has been gone from this earth for a while, but he still lives on in my heart. I still think of him. I keep his picture with his bright smile (smirk) in my house visible for all to see. When I need some advice in tough situations, I still defer to Steve. I will go up to his picture and ask him for his help and guidance. He comes through. I believe his spirit still is around me and in my home. He definitely watches over me and points me in the right direction. Symbolism such as a feather that is sticking up out of nowhere, tells me he is still hanging out here.

Yes, he's gone and I'm sad that I will never play golf with him again, enjoy a Philly cheesesteak or just jab with him, but the fact is, to me, he's not gone. He's in my heart and in my soul. I focus on our great memories and relish the time we had together. Those memories will transcend time and will always be a part of my life. Steve helped me become a better person and in fact, he was one of the best people I ever knew in my life.

RIP Buddy

———»«()»«———

## Steve – By Chad Smith

Steve was my cousin, but he was like a brother to me. I was an only child and I spent a lot of time at the Benning house growing up. Steve's mom took care of me while my parents were at work. The thing I loved about Steve was that whenever I was down, I could talk to him and he would give me one-liners that would always make me feel better. When I got older I could call him and even if he didn't answer the phone, he would call back within an hour or two and I could talk about any problems that I was having, and he would make me feel better. The day I found out that he was gone was not a good day. I found out from a friend that I was working with at the time during the middle of a job we were on. I didn't believe it for a while, I thought they were playing a bad joke on me. It took me a long time to realize that it really did happen. My world stopped at that moment. Steve was the guy I could call about anything and he would help me. I don't have anybody like that anymore. He has left a big hole in my life. The only thing that makes me feel better is that Chase is a lot like him. He has his humor and every time I see him he reminds me more and more of my brother Steve.

———»•«———

## Steve – by Jessica Hayson

How do you even begin to explain grief, or loss, and its effect on you without opening yourself up to feeling hurt all over again?  I willingly share it now for the sake of helping others learn that it's okay to openly grieve the loss of someone that you love.  Even more so, it's okay to feel raw emotions like hurt and sadness and let others see you that way.  I believe that is how we heal.  By opening ourselves up, feeling that hurt, and letting others in so we move forward in a slow and steady process.  It will take time, yes, but it's true when they say time does heal.  Or at least it changes our perspective.

Someone once told me that people are either in your life for a reason, a season, or for life.  Once I met Steve, I always thought it would be for life because we got along so well and laughed like no one was watching (even though I'm convinced everyone was always watching and wondering what in the world we could be laughing at that hard!).  When he died suddenly, I was left to wonder if it was really only a specific season I was meant to have him in my life.  Looking back, it feels like only a small blip on the radar of my life.  It really was.  It was only about three years in total that I knew him, and it wasn't an everyday kind of friendship either.  It was, however, one that no matter how much time passed, it was as if we had just seen each other yesterday and we were simply catching up where we left off the day before. Whether there was a specific reason for it all, I may never know. I was fortunate to count Steve as a friend and it was meaningful to me for that season. For the rest of my life I will hold on to that friendship as one of my most treasured. Just because he is gone, doesn't mean I don't still see him in every day happenings or events. Or laughter. Especially in laughter! One day, something special happened. I shared a meal with my friend who was one a widow and is now remarried, and her son who was once fatherless for a season but now has a new little sister and an amazing stepfather who loves him as deeply as his own father did when he was alive. In that moment, I saw how even in grief and loss amazing things can happen. And when Steve's son and I were laughing together like no one was watching, I knew he was with us and looking down and laughing right along. I almost wished he could be there with us, but then I realized he was.

---

## Steve – by Brian Bengtson

Steve Benning was light. With his light he made everything around him brighter. He was like a star, with his own gravitational pull. People wanted to be around him, it was easy to get pulled into his orbit.

I am incredibly grateful to have shared his light even for a moment. It made my life better, hopefully by telling you about him, I can share his light with you.

Steve was one of the most interesting and fascinating people I have ever met. He was larger than life. His smile was infectious.

He made everything better. If Steve was at your party, it was going to be a good party. If you had the honor of eating dinner with Steve, it was going to be an enjoyable dinner even if the food was terrible.

At Steve and Wendy's wedding it was surprising to see how many friends Steve had. Steve was a great friend. Loyal, trusting, caring and honest.

My first memory of Steve was when Wendy introduced him to me in my college years. I was a protective brother, but I knew right away that we would be lucky to have Steve as a part of our family. I consider him a brother, a friend, and a hero. He was an excited father. He was also an artist. He built beautiful houses with creativity and originality. Steve excelled at bringing dreams and ideas into creation. He was a great carpenter, handyman. I felt like Steve could do anything. When he stayed with you he was the perfect guest. He cleaned the house, made breakfast, fixed the door, adjusted the pool pump and played spider man with my son. Our family loved Steve and even though he was my brother- in-law, I thought of him as a close friend. Everybody did.

I had the fortune of living near Steve when he and Wendy moved to California. He was incredibly gracious, forgiving, and accepting of me and I always appreciated it. He was there for me when I struggled, he backed me up when I needed it. He was incredibly caring. He was always smiling.

After Steve's death I went into a personal tailspin. His death affected me deeply. I gave up on life for a while. I stopped brushing my teeth. I stopped cleaning my face. I wore the same pair of clothes for weeks. I could not sleep, or I would sleep forever. Everything reminded me of Steve, every conversation with my dad or sister would bring it up. I could not leave the house.

Why would God let this happen? Why is life so unfair? I could not forget it, I could not let it go.

I would continually think about Chase, Steve's beautiful son. He was so young. He would never get to know his father, hear his laugh, feel his love. This overwhelmed me. I began drinking again. Anything to escape from this. I would feel guilty that I was still alive while Steve was gone. Steve deserved to live more than me. He was a better person.

It seemed at one point that this utter devastation, regret, and hopelessness would continue forever. After some time, I realized the lessons and experiences that Steve had left behind were a gift. The gift of his graciousness, his sense of humor, his bigger than life personality were very special. I think of him every day. The idea of Steve never died, he left an incredible legacy, and special memories. It is a reminder of how short life is, I am grateful for the time I got to spend with him.

One day while I was caught up in a memory of Steve deep in the throes of depression and hopelessness, I heard Steve's voice whisper in my ear, "Be grateful, enjoy the moment, everything is going to be OK!"

Wendy says that when she sees feathers it is a sign from Steve. Once she said that, I began to see feathers all the time. Just today as I started to write this, I went out to get the mail and a feather rested on my front porch.

My life is infinitely better because Steve was in it, even for that brief time. He taught me how to live and love. In his death I learned to love life with integrity and honesty. Steve taught me that life is a piece of art and that tomorrow was not guaranteed. He taught me how precious our lives are. He taught me about gratitude.

When a star in the universe has burnt out, we still see its light for years after its death. Steve is that star shining in the sky. His light remains.

I will never forget him.

———⚫———

### Steve – by Gustavo Peralta ("G-man" to Steve)

I love cooking. Cooking for family and friends is a great way to share something special with the ones you love. Cooking comes with a price…doing dishes. It is a methodical task and my mind travels in all directions when I do them. It goes to different places getting lost between plates and silverware. I was doing dishes that late afternoon at Huntington Beach, the place I shared with Kristin. We had some friends for Thanksgiving. One thing I remember is the dishwasher door wide open like a bridge in a castle inviting the dirty peasants to take a bath. I told you my mind go places. Then I saw Steve goofing around and walking back into the door, he fell over it like he meant to do that and stood up pretending like as nothing happened. But it did, and all of us saw it. He knew he was caught so his attitude switched quickly as he was the one that won gold in the most difficult event in the dishwashing Olympic Games.

Steve had the gift of turning the uneventful into special, the difficult into something easy. He could make you laugh and he could make fun of you without an ounce of malice. He even challenged people to surpass his accomplishment. Of course, nobody accepted, so he declared himself the winner.

A few years later I was doing dishes in our new place in San Clemente. Kristin's phone rang. She picked it up and went outside, to the backyard. I knew something was wrong, I thought something happened to her family. I went outside. It was Bennie, she said, Steve is dead. We were both speechless, we hugged without saying a word. We went inside, trying to make sense of what we just learned. I keep doing dishes as if I can go somewhere else, but it did not work. Time went by, I kept cooking and doing dishes. For some time, I tried to ignore the open door of the dishwasher, I guess to avoid the sadness, but I finally let it happen. Not sure how long it took, but after a while, it was not there anymore. From time to time I do look at the open door with a smile in my face, then I go back to the task making sure the plastic spaceships, Tupperware, don't land in the bottom rack to avoid heat damage. Love you, Dirty. G Man.

56299984R20083

Made in the USA
Columbia, SC
26 April 2019